HIKE THE PARKS

MESA VERDE NATIONAL PARK & BEYOND

HIKE THE PARKS

BEST DAY HIKES, WALKS, AND SIGHTS

MESA VERDE NATIONAL PARK & BEYOND

COURTNEY JOHNSON

MOUNTAINEERS BOOKS

MOUNTAINEERS BOOKS is dedicated to the exploration, preservation, and enjoyment of outdoor and wilderness areas.

1001 SW Klickitat Way, Suite 201, Seattle, WA 98134
800-553-4453, www.mountaineersbooks.org

Printed in China
First edition, 2025

Design: Jen Grable
Layout: McKenzie Long, Cardinal Innovative
Cartographer: Mike Powers
All photographs by the author unless credited otherwise
Cover photographs, front: *View from Long House on Wetherill Mesa in Mesa Verde National Park* (SCGerding, iStock); back, *on the way to Geyser Spring (Hike 23)*
Frontispiece: *Intriguing rock formations can be found along Spruce Canyon Loop (Hike 6).*
Last page: *Aspen trees line many sections of the trail to Geyser Spring (Hike 23).*

Leave No Trace Seven Principles © Leave No Trace, www.LNT.org

Library of Congress record is available at https://lccn.loc.gov/2025012102.

Mountaineers Books titles may be purchased for corporate, educational, or other promotional sales, and our authors are available for a wide range of events. For information on special discounts or booking an author, contact our customer service at 800-553-4453 or mbooks@mountaineersbooks.org.

Printed on FSC®-certified materials

MIX
Paper | Supporting responsible forestry
FSC® C188448

ISBN (paperback): 978-1-68051-738-5
ISBN (ebook): 978-1-68051-739-2

An independent nonprofit publisher since 1960

CONTENTS

PART 2: MANCOS, CORTEZ, AND DOLORES

MANCOS

CORTEZ

DOLORES

PART 3: CANYONS OF THE ANCIENTS NATIONAL MONUMENT

PLEASANT VIEW AREA

SAND CANYON AND ROCK CREEK

PART 4: HOVENWEEP NATIONAL MONUMENT

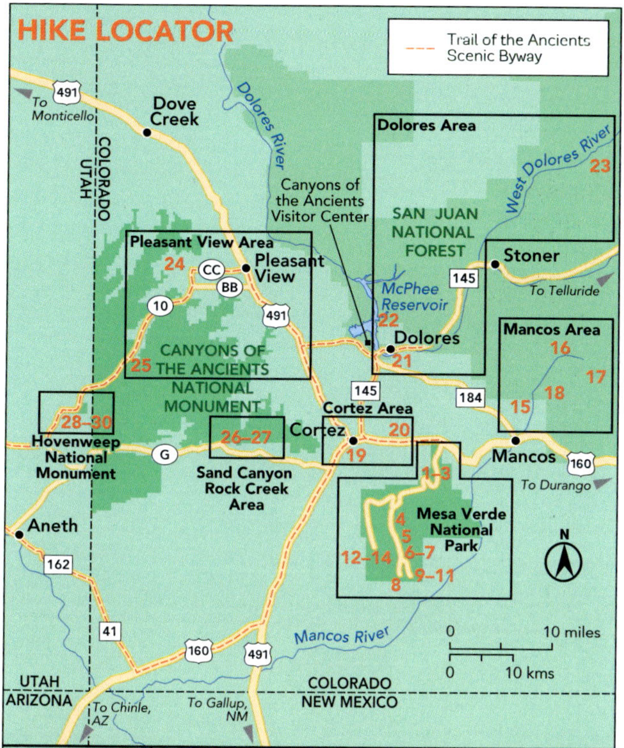
HIKE LOCATOR
Trail of the Ancients Scenic Byway
To Monticello
491
Dove Creek
COLORADO
UTAH
Dolores River
Canyons of the Ancients Visitor Center
Dolores Area
West Dolores River
23
SAN JUAN NATIONAL FOREST
Pleasant View Area
24
CC
BB
Pleasant View
10
491
Stoner
145
To Telluride
McPhee Reservoir
22
Dolores
21
CANYONS OF THE ANCIENTS NATIONAL MONUMENT
25
Mancos Area
16
17
18
15
145
184
Cortez Area
28–30
Hovenweep National Monument
G
26–27
Sand Canyon Rock Creek Area
Cortez
20
19
Mancos
160
To Durango
1–3
Mesa Verde National Park
4
5
6–7
12–14
9–11
8
Aneth
162
N
41
160
491
Mancos River
0
10 miles
0
10 kms
UTAH
ARIZONA
COLORADO
NEW MEXICO
To Chinle, AZ
To Gallup, NM

REGION OVERVIEW
WYOMING
80
Salt Lake City
25
76
NEB.
Denver
15
UTAH
70
70
COLORADO
KANSAS
NEVADA
191
50
MESA VERDE NATIONAL PARK
550
160
Durango
89
25
OKLA.
Las Vegas
64
ARIZONA
160
491
TEXAS
550
89
191
15
40
40
Flagstaff
Albuquerque
CALIFORNIA
NEW MEXICO
N
17
0
100 miles
10
Phoenix
San Diego
25
0
100 kms
8

HIKES AT A GLANCE

HIKE	DISTANCE miles (km)	ELEVATION GAIN feet (m)	HIGH POINT feet (m)	DIFFICULTY
PART 1: MESA VERDE NATIONAL PARK				
MOREFIELD VILLAGE				
1. Prater Ridge Loop	7.8 (19)	675 (205)	8422 (2567)	Challenging
2. Knife Edge	2 (3.2)	62 (18)	7800 (2380)	Easy
3. Point Lookout	2.2 (3.5)	400 (121)	8427 (2568)	Moderate
MESA TOP RUINS ROAD				
4. Far View Sites	1 (1.6)	185 (56)	7750 (2362)	Easy
5. Farming Terrace	0.5 (0.8)	75 (22)	7108 (2166)	Easy
CHAPIN MESA				
6. Spruce Canyon Loop	2.4 (3.9)	558 (170)	8427 (2166)	Moderate
7. Petroglyph Point Trail	2.4 (3.8)	174 (53)	6953 (2119)	Moderate
8. Square Tower House	1 (1.6)	100 (30)	6857 (2090)	Moderate
9. Cliff Palace Overview	0.4 (0.6)	115 (35)	6800 (2072)	Moderate
10. Balcony House	0.4 (0.6)	150 (45)	6800 (2072)	Moderate
11. Soda Canyon Overlook	1.2 (1.9)	173 (52)	6850 (2090)	Easy

OPPOSITE: *The Knife Edge Trail (Hike 2) has a knife edge appearance as it follows the bluff.*

HIKE	DISTANCE miles (km)	ELEVATION GAIN feet (m)	HIGH POINT feet (m)	DIFFICULTY
WETHERILL MESA				
12. Step House Loop	1 (1.6)	100 (52)	7300 (2225)	Moderate
13. Nordenskiöld Site No. 16 Trail	2 (3.2)	95 (29)	7300 (2225)	Easy
14. Long House Loop	4.3 (6.9)	285 (86)	7218 (2200)	Easy
PART 2: MANCOS, CORTEZ, AND DOLORES				
MANCOS				
15. Mancos State Park Loop	4.7 (7.5)	400 (121)	8245 (2513)	Easy
16. Big Al Trail	1.2 (1.9)	77 (23.5)	8980 (2737)	Easy
17. Sharkstooth Pass	3 (5)	1035 (320)	11,945 (3640)	Moderate
18. Ramparts Loop	5.4 (8.7)	1079 (329)	9344 (2848)	Moderate
CORTEZ				
19. Hawkins Preserve Loop	3 (5)	112 (34)	6100 (1859)	Easy
20. Trust and Hippie House Loop	6.2 (9.9)	320 (97.5)	6425 (1958)	Moderate
DOLORES				
21. Dolores River Trail	2.9 (4.6)	29 (8.8)	6936 (2114)	Easy
22. McPhee Overlook	12 (19)	1400 (426)	7230 (2203)	Challenging
23. Geyser Spring	3 (5)	500 (152)	9100 (2773)	Easy to moderate

HIKE	DISTANCE miles (km)	ELEVATION GAIN feet (m)	HIGH POINT feet (m)	DIFFICULTY
PART 3: CANYONS OF THE ANCIENTS NATIONAL MONUMENT				
PLEASANT VIEW AREA				
24. Lowry Pueblo	0.3 (0.4)	25 (7.6)	6736 (2053)	Easy
25. Painted Hand Pueblo	0.8 (1.3)	150 (45)	6079 (1852)	Easy
SAND CANYON AND ROCK CREEK				
26. East Rock Creek Loop	7.2 (11)	705 (214)	5850 (1783)	Moderate
27. Sand Canyon	12 (19.3)	1960 (597)	6863 (2091)	Challenging
PART 4: HOVENWEEP NATIONAL MONUMENT				
28. Square Tower Loop	2 (3.2)	220 (67)	5249 (1599)	Easy
29. Holly Group	7 (11)	646 (196)	8200 (2499)	Moderate
30. Horseshoe and Hackberry	1.4 (2.2)	91 (27)	5525 (1684)	Easy

VISITING MESA VERDE NATIONAL PARK AND BEYOND

Southwestern Colorado boasts an incredible density of archaeological sites—from villages and kivas to shrines and agricultural fields. Each one provides insight into the lives of the Ancestral Puebloan, Navajo, Apache, and Ute peoples. In the Four Corners region, the 116-mile (187 km) Trail of the Ancients Scenic Byway connects many of the hikes in this book: Lowry Pueblo in Canyons of the Ancients National Monument, the stone towers of Hovenweep National Monument, locations around the towns of Cortez and Dolores, and the area's centerpiece, Mesa Verde National Park.

The national park and monuments, along with the towns of Mancos, Cortez, and Dolores, are sandwiched between San Juan National Forest to the northeast and Indian Country to the south and southwest—the Southern Ute, Ute Mountain, and Navajo Indian Reservations. Arising in the peaks of the national forest, rivers including the Dolores and Mancos flow west through the arid high plateaus of Southwestern Colorado. A handful of hikes among the forests and rivers, in areas such as Mancos State Park and McPhee Reservoir, contrast with the spectacular mesas, rock formations, and washes of canyon country.

OPPOSITE: *A view of Square Tower including the Crow's Nest*

MESA VERDE NATIONAL PARK

Located in the transition zone between the Rocky Mountains and the desert plateau, Mesa Verde National Park is one of the smallest national parks in the United States, at 52,485 acres (21,240 hectares)—81 square miles (210 sq km). Spanish for "green table," Mesa Verde was originally named by European settlers in 1859. In 1906, it was declared a national park by then president Theodore Roosevelt. It is sometimes referred to as the pyramids of North America.

Within the boundaries of Mesa Verde National Park, visitors can view six hundred cliff dwellings and five thousand archaeological sites. The Ancestral Puebloan people called the place home for more than seven centuries, from CE 600 to 1300. They made clothes, farmed the land, built shelter, and created laws and customs. One of the oldest national parks, Mesa Verde contains one of the largest archaeological preserves in the United States and was named a UNESCO World Heritage site in 1978. In April 2021, the National Park Service and the International Dark-Sky Association announced Mesa Verde National Park as the 100th International Dark Sky Park.

MANCOS STATE PARK

Just north of the town of Mancos, Mancos State Park encompasses Jackson Gulch Reservoir and Lakeview Ridge, with trails inside the park as well as access to trails into San Juan National Forest. The reservoir on the West Mancos River was created in 1948 and the park was established in 1987, offering camping and hiking as well as sailing, boating, and fishing. Wildlife includes Abert's squirrels, mule deer, and many bird species, from broad-tailed hummingbirds to bald eagles.

HAWKINS PRESERVE

Hawkins Preserve is located within the city limits of the town of Cortez. In the 1990s, Jack Hawkins donated 122 acres (49

THE KNIFE EDGE ROAD

The first route used by motor vehicle traffic to access the top of the mesa within the park, Knife Edge Road was completed in 1923 as a part of making the park more accessible to visitors. However, the road was the site of many vehicle accidents, landslides, and rockfalls; eventually the frequent road closures and yearly maintenance became too costly for the park. After the Morefield-Prater Tunnel replaced the Knife Edge Road in 1957, the road bed was turned into the Knife Edge Trail, which visitors enjoy today.

hectares) of land to the Cortez Cultural Center to preserve archaeological resources including the Hawkins Pueblo. The land had been occupied during the Pueblo I and Pueblo II period around AD 900. In 2004, the Cortez Cultural Center created a conservation easement held by the Montezuma Land Conservancy to protect the land. The preserve features more than 200 species of plants as well as activities from climbing to hiking, with over 3 miles (4.8 km) of trails open from dusk until dawn daily.

CANYONS OF THE ANCIENTS NATIONAL MONUMENT

Located in the Four Corners region of Southwestern Colorado, Canyons of the Ancients National Monument is an outdoor museum of sorts. This Bureau of Land Management preserve was created on June 9, 2000. There are more than eight thousand marked sites across the 174,000-acre (70,415 hectare) monument lands. Aside from Painted Hand Pueblo, Sand Canyon, and the pueblos of Lowry, other sites including pueblos, towers, and kivas are unmarked and unrestored. Canyons of the Ancients has the highest known archaeological site density in the United States, with an estimated thirty thousand sites in the monument area. To make the most of a visit here, stop first at the Canyons of the Ancients Visitor Center (formerly the Anasazi Heritage Center) near Dolores.

HOVENWEEP NATIONAL MONUMENT

The word *hovenweep* means "deserted valley" in Ute/Paiute. Created March 2, 1923, Hovenweep National Monument contains six prehistoric villages built from CE 1200 to 1300. An estimated twenty-five hundred people lived in the prehistoric villages. The monument is unique because it stretches across two states—Southeastern Utah and Southwestern Colorado—on the Cajon Mesa of the Great Sage Plain.

Four of these villages—Holly, Hackberry, Horseshoe, and Cutthroat Castle—are in the state of Colorado. The other two villages—Square Tower and Cajon—are located in Utah. The villages contain multilevel towers (whose function is unknown) and kivas. The villages were abandoned in the thirteenth century as the Ancestral Puebloans moved south. In July 2014, the International Dark-Sky Association designated Hovenweep National Monument as an International Dark Sky Park.

HUMAN HISTORY

Most of the history of Southwestern Colorado follows the model of the American Southwest, from Indigenous habitation and European settlers to the establishment of areas as national parks or monuments to today's modern environment. The original inhabitants of the area were Ancestral Puebloan people, along with more nomadic Indigenous peoples who farmed, hunted, traded, and established roots within the canyons and land.

With no definitive proof, many historians and archaeologists believe that drought and difficult farming conditions forced the Ancestral Puebloans to move away from the Four Corners region of Utah and Colorado, heading southeast to

UTE MOUNTAIN TRIBAL PARK

If you're traveling the Trail of the Ancients Scenic Byway, plan a visit to the Ute Mountain Tribal Park. The hike and tour at this park are not included in this book due to the park's commercial photography restrictions. Additionally, no self-guided tours are permitted; you must book either a half-day or full-day tour. The tours, led by Ute Indian guides, are a fully immersive experience, making a visit to the park worth your time.

present-day New Mexico and Arizona. Safety from raiding nomadic peoples is also a theory on why the area was largely abandoned in CE 1300.

After the Ancestral Puebloans migrated, evidence shows the area was occupied by hunter-gatherers who today are the ancestors of the Navajo and Ute peoples. With the arrival of Spanish explorers in the middle to late 1700s, the effects of exploration began to impact the Indigenous cultures. While the explorers didn't settle in the area, they brought disease, weapons, and governmental control that led to the displacement of the Ute and Navajo peoples. Mineral prospectors and explorers took over most of the area in the 1800s, leading to further decline of Indigenous inhabitants.

FEDERAL PROTECTION FOR THE PARKS

In an effort to protect and preserve the cultural heritage of the Ancestral Puebloans, Mesa Verde National Park was designated a national park in 1906. Furthermore, it was granted added protection the same year with the passing of the Federal Antiquities Act to protect all cultural remains across the country. However, park rangers did not stay onsite in the winter, and the superintendent lived a town over, in Mancos. With little services, the park didn't receive many visitors, but

TIMELINE FOR MESA VERDE NATIONAL PARK

1884: Prospector S. E. Osborn enters Balcony House in lower Soda Canyon on March 20, 1884. His name can be seen on the wall today.

1886: On December 12, an article in the *Denver Tribune Republican* suggests the area be designated as a national park.

1901: On February 22, a bill is introduced in Congress to create "Colorado Cliff Dwellings National Park," but it does not get past the Public Lands Committee.

1901 to 1903: Two new bills introduced to the House of Representatives of the Fifty-Seventh Congress to establish a park do not get past the Public Lands Committee.

1903: Secretary of the Interior negotiates the Mesa Verde tract with the Ute Indians.

1903 to 1905: Two new bills are introduced in the Fifty-Eighth Congress to establish "Colorado Cliff Dwellings National Park," with little progress.

1905: A bill creating Mesa Verde National Park is presented to the Fifty-Ninth Congress. It is signed on June 29, 1906, by President Theodore Roosevelt to "preserve the works of man," creating one of the very first national parks.

1906: The Antiquities Act is passed on June 8, making it a federal crime to destroy any building or collect any prehistoric or historic object on federally owned land.

1978: Mesa Verde National Park is designated as a UNESCO World Heritage site, offering further protection.

that meant it also had very little protection from looters and "potholers."

In 1921, Jesse Nusbaum was chosen as the new park superintendent by the National Park Service—the first time a trained archaeologist was in charge of Mesa Verde. Along the rim of Spruce Tree Canyon he built administrative structures that helped staff be on the premises to protect the park. This administrative district on Chapin Mesa was listed as a National Historic Landmark in 1987. Nusbaum stepped down as superintendent in 1931 but continued as an archaeological consultant for the National Park Service to help in alterations to buildings at Mesa Verde. Further protection was granted in 1978 when Mesa Verde was recognized as a UNESCO World Heritage site.

Today, the national parks and monuments use compliance archaeologists to continue preservation, including one I worked with while writing this guidebook. A compliance archaeologist travels to parks to ensure that agencies comply with federal and state laws protecting cultural resources. They monitor restoration projects, construction jobs that include ground disturbances, and the closing of sites.

GEOLOGY

The geology of Southwestern Colorado has a long history from seaway to sand dunes. The Colorado Plateau encompasses 240,000 square miles (621,597 sq km) and covers the area where the thirty hikes in this book travel.

One of the features of this area is the Great Sage Plain, a 1500-square-mile (3,885 sq km) plateau stretching west from the San Juan Mountains to the Abajo and La Sal Mountains in Utah. Its southern extent is found at Ute Mountain and Mesa Verde National Park, and its center is Lowry Pueblo in Canyons of the Ancients National Monument.

MESA VERDE NATIONAL PARK

Some 100 million years ago, the Western Interior Seaway washed over the area surrounding Mesa Verde in what is now Colorado. Due to climate change in the Cretaceous period, the sea retreated and grew many times. Depositing Dakota

Turtleback weathering along with desert varnish along Petroglyph Point Trail (Hike 7)

Sandstone, it created the base of Montezuma Valley, which extends southwest of Cortez into northeastern Arizona.

As the sea moved westward, it deposited Mancos Shale, visible from the Knife Edge Trail in Mesa Verde. Within the shale are fossils of ammonites, shark teeth, and clams. The shale creates a gray layer of rock at the base of the mesa of Montezuma Valley.

Three different formations known as the Mesaverde Group create the layers above the Mancos Shale. The Point Lookout Formation was the last formation created by the sea. Directly above the Mancos Shale, the formation is tan or buff sandstone. It created alcoves that were not known to be used by the Ancestral Puebloans. The Knife Edge Trail and Point Lookout are two places in the park to see this layer up close.

After the sea departed, flat plains remained. Decaying plants and organic material created a fine-grain shale known as the Menefee Formation. This black and dark brown shale on top of the Point Lookout Sandstone can be seen at the park's Geologic Overlook. The last formation, Cliff House Sandstone, is what the Ancestral Puebloans used to build cliff dwellings. This layer is visible at any viewpoint of the dwellings and within the dwellings themselves.

Throughout Mesa Verde, geological features include seep springs created from the juncture of two layers: Cliff House Sandstone and Menefee Shale. Moss and ferns grow in the seeps today. Significant to the Ancestral Puebloans, solution rills formed from acidic rain can be seen at the Sun Temple Viewpoint on Chapin Mesa. Soil known as loess still covers the mesa top. Turtleback weathering (pillow-like or turtle shell appearance of rock eroded into cracks and rounded tops) and concretions also are features found in the park.

CANYONS OF THE ANCIENTS NATIONAL MONUMENT

The land encompassing Canyons of the Ancients National Monument can be traced back to the Cretaceous period. On the edge of the Colorado Plateau, the upper layers of rock from the Jurassic and Cretaceous periods create the canyon walls of the monument.

Navajo Sandstone, also known as slickrock, is the lowest rock layer from the Lower Jurassic period. It was transported from the once Ancestral Appalachian Mountains by wind and water to a giant sand sea. The Carmel Formation is the second layer, consisting of limestone, mudstone, and gypsum deposited into the seaway by ocean currents. Within the Middle Jurassic, the Entrada Sandstone layer was created

The rim of McElmo Canyon is visible off in the distance from Patrick's Point.

from local materials transported by wind and is identified as a red layer of slickrock.

The oldest rocks of the monument are found within McElmo Canyon. Bent due to tremendous pressure, sedimentary rock created the McElmo Dome. Mississippian rock found in and around McElmo Dome is home to one of the largest deposits of carbon dioxide found in the United States. The highest peaks in the monument include Cajon Mesa, Mockingbird Mesa, and White Rock.

HOVENWEEP NATIONAL MONUMENT

The drainage of water from the San Juan River along the Colorado Plateau carved the winding canyons in Hovenweep. On Cajon Mesa, the lowest elevation is 4900 feet (1494 m) at Cajon Ruin while the highest is 6800 feet (2073 m) at Cutthroat Castle.

There are two main layers of rock viewable at Hovenweep. The lowest rock layer, the Burro Canyon Formation, is composed of sandstone, mudrock, and green shale. Within the formation are quartzite and limestone cobbles and pebbles. During the Cretaceous period, this formation was deposited by the seaway. The Ancient Puebloans used these rocks to create arrowheads and tools. This layer is most visible on the trail to Cutthroat Castle and crossing the canyon on the Square Tower Loop trail.

The top layer at the monument is Dakota Sandstone, composed of beds of coal, mudstone, and yellowish-gray sandstone. The coastal plains and swamp that remained after the sea moved westward, this layer was deposited during the late Cretaceous period. Ancient Puebloans used this sandstone to make manos and metates for grinding corn and grains and to create the castles and towers you can view at Hovenweep today.

Ephemeral pools and seeps in the monument show where the water collected after the sea retreated. When rain falls or snow melts, these areas collect water today.

FLORA AND FAUNA

Covering four biotic zones, the land around Mesa Verde contains a large array of plant and animal species. There are over 640 species of trees and plants in the national park. Most plants are endemic, from Oregon grape to snowberry and Utah juniper.

Wild rhubarb lines the Holly Trail (Hike 29).

FLORA

The Ancestral Puebloans harvested a very large number of edible plants that grow wild. As we would say today, "The land was their grocery store." In fact, the Basketmakers and Cliff Dwellers came to rely on more than 160 species of edible plants in Mesa Verde as a part of their diet, for medicine, tools, and fibers for weaving baskets, ropes, clothing, and blankets.

Visitors can still see these plants today lining the trails in and around Mesa Verde. Grab a pamphlet and go for a hike on the Knife Edge Trail, the original road into the park, for an educational look into the flora and fauna of the area.

Shrub-steppe community. The lower elevations are a mix of sagebrush and other shrubs, from Mormon tea to yucca. The lower elevation of Hovenweep National Monument brings a smaller variety of plants than in Mesa Verde National Park. Within the 325 plant species, there are many of the "grocery store" plants that the Ancestral Puebloans used in everyday life, including serviceberry and Mormon tea. Sagebrush and rabbitbrush spread across the trails.

The Weidmeyer's admiral butterfly is often spotted along the trail to Geyser Spring (Hike 23).

Pygmy forest. The forest of smaller juniper and piñon pine is the second zone in Mesa Verde. Mountain shrubs from Gambel oak to several species of mahogany bring color in the fall.

Coniferous forest. At the highest elevations, visitors find ponderosa pine and Douglas-fir. Canyons of the Ancients National Monument ranges in elevation between 5400 and 7000 feet (1646 and 2134 m). The high desert is home to a large variety of wildflowers, from Mojave kingcup cactus to thistle and yucca.

Riparian habitats. Along the rivers in this region, you'll find cottonwoods and willows. The Mancos River flowing though Mesa Verde creates a riparian zone in the park.

FAUNA

A variety of species—including sixteen species of reptiles, two hundred species of birds, and seventy-four of mammals—can be found within Mesa Verde National Park.

Mammals. Some mammals are migratory. Bats, mountain lions, and an increasing number of bears now call Mesa Verde home. Bobcats, jackrabbits, foxes, and mule deer are some of the mammals that live in Canyons of the Ancients National Monument. Ten species of bats shelter in Hovenweep National Monument. Mammals are scarce in the monument, although mule deer, mountain lions, and coyotes roam the acreage.

Reptiles. Five species of snakes live within Mesa Verde, including the prairie rattlesnake, the smooth green snake, and the western striped racer. Horned lizards or sagebrush lizards (also called sagebrush swifts) often can be found sunning on rocks or racing past you on a trail. Spiny and leopard lizards and Mesa Verde night snakes are some of the reptiles visitors may see in Canyons of the Ancients. Collared lizards are very common within Hovenweep National Monument. Common side-blotched lizards (utas) are frequent greeters at Mesa Verde and Hovenweep.

Collared lizards frequent many of these trails.

Birds. Some birds are migratory, including hummingbirds. Birds of prey from kestrels to golden eagles are plentiful in Canyons of the Ancients. Ravens are very common within Hovenweep.

Endangered species. There are endangered or threatened animals and plants, such as the Mesa Verde cactus, within the national park and monuments. Insects such as the rare protected black swallowtail butterfly rely on native plants like the Mesa Verde wild parsleys. The Mexican spotted owl is also on the endangered species list within the park. Rare fish and reptiles, from the Mesa Verde night snake to the long-nosed leopard lizard, are also under threat.

THREATS TO THE AREA

Since rancher Richard Wetherill and his four younger brothers discovered sites in the cliffs of Mesa Verde in 1889, the area has been threatened. While protections, including national park or monument status, cover some of the threats, preservation remains of the utmost importance.

Erosion and weather are concerns within the park and monuments. As the soil erodes due to weather and other

CLIMATE CHANGE IN THE MESA VERDE REGION

While the parks and monuments use controlled burns for mitigation, out-of-control wildfires have ravaged parts of each park and monument including near areas where archaeologists have uncovered artifacts and sites from the Ancestral Puebloans. Such wildfires have been increasing as climate change continues. In 2000 the loss of vegetation in a fire at Mesa Verde uncovered stone walls, adding an additional layer to the difficulty of preserving the area while also maintaining safety.

Invasive species, including cheatgrass, have encroached into areas of the park, monuments, and drought-stricken places, competing with native species. With drought and invasive species taking over, soil erosion has altered vegetation.

An increase in temperatures has created a decrease of water levels in springs, rivers, and forests, affecting flora and fauna in the areas covered in this guidebook. These temperature swings also have damaging effects on cliff faces and dwellings that erode quicker due to the heat.

sources, the sites continue to be fragile. Water seepage can also affect the stability of the structures, while plants like moss can damage the structures if they grow within the sites. Over time, the structures lose stability, which can cause closure (Spruce Tree Canyon in Mesa Verde) or restoration projects. An increase in road building for oil and gas extraction and an overall increase in car travel in the area has posed an ongoing threat to the fragility of the area.

With the possible coal mine expansion of the King II mine within 10 miles (16 km) of Mesa Verde National Park and oil and gas exploration near the monuments, air quality is of concern for visitors, plant life, and animal life within the protected lands. Construction and extraction at oil and gas interests also add to air quality issues.

Although federal protections against vandalism and looting are in place, funding for parks and monuments continues to decrease. Thus, the ability to police activity by visitors is more difficult. Since the sites were first discovered, thousands of artifacts have been taken for sale or personal collections. Carving into rock and digging up prehistoric charcoal to draw or write names are some of the most frequent acts of vandalism that occur.

Cattle grazing operations are a concern in Canyons of the Ancients National Monument. Cattle damage the frangible cryptobiotic soil and fragile stone walls within the monument. Trampling of delicate plants is another concern. Livestock also affect waterways within the monument. Seeds from invasive plants attach to cattle and spread weeds such as cheatgrass and knapweed.

Invasive plants are a threatening concern for preservation within the park and monuments. Native plants are losing the space and sunlight they need to continue to thrive. Each entity works hard to keep invasive plants from taking over. Flags may be placed along the sides of trails identifying native and nonnative species in the ongoing effort to control noxious weeds and other invaders, including musk thistle and cheatgrass.

OPPOSITE: *Kids will love the cool rock formations along many of these trails, including this one on Petroglyph Point Trail (Hike 7).*

PLANNING YOUR TRIP

To maximize your trip to Southwestern Colorado, it is important to be prepared. This chapter will help you plan for a successful and enjoyable trip.

VISITOR CENTERS

Most of the places this guidebook covers have a visitor center, including Mancos State Park. These facilities provide a wealth of information as well as services such as maps, restrooms, and informative staff.

MESA VERDE NATIONAL PARK

Mesa Verde National Park features one visitor center and a museum. The park entrance is south of US Highway 160 between Cortez and Mancos, and just south of the highway exit is the Mesa Verde National Park Visitor and Research Center. Here is where you must purchase tour tickets to visit Balcony House and Cliff Palace on Chapin Mesa and Long House on Wetherill Mesa. If you are looking for walk-up permits for cliff-dwelling tours, the visitor center is where you can find out if any last-minute tickets are available. The park entrance station, where you'll find restrooms, is a bit farther south on the park road, about 1 mile (1.6 km) from the highway.

Both Far View Terrace and Spruce Tree Terrace have a cafe, gift shop, and restrooms. Chapin Mesa Archaeological

OPPOSITE: *The Holly Group Trail takes you from the campgrounds across the canyon.*

Museum is located 20 miles (32 km) south of the park entrance. At both Far View and Chapin Mesa, you can learn about park history, view artifacts, buy souvenirs, and chat with park rangers about maximizing your visit.

At Wetherill Mesa, there is a cafe and a ranger station, where visitors can ask questions or get recommendations.

CANYONS OF THE ANCIENTS NATIONAL MONUMENT

Canyons of the Ancients Visitor Center and Museum is located at 27501 State Highway 184 in the town of Dolores. The visitor center features a museum and gift shop. Begin your visit here to maximize your time in this sprawling national monument. Featuring a collection of more than 3.5 million items, the museum exhibits the culture of life in the Four Corners region for Ancestral Puebloans; Pueblo, Ute, and Navajo Indians; and Anglo settlers.

A tour of this museum is a sensory experience. Visitors have an opportunity to touch stone points, pottery, and other real artifacts. Interactive computer-based exhibits highlight archaeology and history of the Four Corners. A replica pit house shows how household furnishings have changed. Learn how archaeologists use tree rings to date findings.

MESA VERDE VOICES

Before your visit to Southwestern Colorado—or along the drive to or in the park—the free *Mesa Verde Voices* podcast on Soundcloud is well worth listening to. Beginning with three pilot episodes in 2017, there are six seasons that connect "modern people to those who lived in the Mesa Verde Region hundreds of years ago." The podcast helps you build a deeper understanding of the significance of the area, from the importance of corn to learning about rock art, in the long history of the United States.

Just outside the museum are two archaeological sites: the Dominguez and Escalante Pueblos. There is also an extensive research library, a half-mile nature trail, and places to enjoy a picnic lunch or dinner.

HOVENWEEP NATIONAL MONUMENT

The visitor center at Hovenweep National Monument is located in Utah east of the monument entrance off US 191 between Blanding and Bluff; the park road heads west 30 miles (48 km) to almost reach the Utah-Colorado state line. You will find the visitor center in the monument's main unit, Square Tower Group. Rangers can answer questions, and exhibits detail past life. The park store has items from books and maps to souvenirs.

HAWKINS PRESERVE

Since 2000, the Cortez Cultural Center has stewarded Hawkins Preserve as well as provided cultural activities in Cortez, such as a spring birding festival, an autumn harvest and culinary month, and tours combining birding, archaeology, ecology, and history. Located in a historical building in Cortez, the center has a coffee shop, gallery, and gift shop. The preserve is 1.5 miles (2.4 km) south of the Cultural Center.

CAMPGROUNDS AND LODGING

Mesa Verde National Park contains one campground and one lodge. Canyons of the Ancients National Monument has only backcountry camping. Hovenweep National Monument has one campground. Mancos State Park features two campgrounds and two reservable yurts that are open year-round.

MESA VERDE NATIONAL PARK

Morefield Campground is located at mile marker 4 (6.4 km) south of US 160 in Mesa Verde National Park. It features 267 sites total, including 15 RV sites with full electric

KEY STATISTICS

MESA VERDE NATIONAL PARK

- Established: June 29, 1906
- Acreage: 52,000 acres (21,043 hectares)
- Designated as wilderness: 15 percent (8100 acres; 3277 hectares)
- Low point: Spruce Canyon floor, 6000 feet (1828 m)
- High point: Park Point Lookout, 8572 feet (2162 m)
- Average annual visitation: 565,000

CANYONS OF THE ANCIENTS NATIONAL MONUMENT

- Established: June 9, 2000
- Acreage: 174,000 acres (70,415 hectares)
- Designated as wilderness: 18–20 percent (31,320–34,800 acres; 12,674–14,083 hectares)
- Low point: Sand Canyon bottom, 5400 feet (1645 m)
- High point: Sand Canyon Pueblo, 6808 feet (1981 m)
- Average annual visitation: 45,000

HOVENWEEP NATIONAL MONUMENT

- Established: March 2, 1923
- Acreage: 785 acres (317 hectares)
- Designated as wilderness: None
- Low point: Cinder Cone, 5100 feet (1554 m)
- High point: Square Tower Group, 5400 feet (1645 m)
- Average annual visitation: 40,000

hookups, and 17 group sites. The campground is open seasonally between early May and the beginning of November, weather dependent, with limited services in early May and mid-October until it closes. Sites are reserved through recreation.gov up to six months in advance. The filling-service village at the campground includes a camp store for registration, food, supplies, gas, showers, and laundry.

The seasonal Knife Edge Cafe provides an all-you-can-eat pancake breakfast. Evening programs take place at the amphitheater.

The Far View Lodge is located at mile marker 15 (24 km) south of US 160 in Mesa Verde National Park. It is open seasonally from mid-April through mid-October. Its 150 rooms each offer a view into three states on clear days as well as nighttime stars.

CANYONS OF THE ANCIENTS NATIONAL MONUMENT

Camping is allowed only in the backcountry areas of Canyons of the Ancients National Monument. No camping permit is needed. Campfires are prohibited in archaeological sites and within 300 feet (91 m) of water sources—ponds, springs, streams—and developed areas including trails, kiosks, and parking areas. No camping is allowed at front-country recreation areas: the Sand Canyon and Rock Creek area, Pueblo sites, and all trailheads.

HOVENWEEP NATIONAL MONUMENT

Hovenweep National Monument Campground is located a quarter mile from the visitor center on the Utah side of the monument. The thirty-one campsites are first-come first-serve. A few sites can accommodate recreational vehicles up to 36 feet (11 m); one site is designated wheelchair accessible. The campground is open year-round.

MANCOS STATE PARK

The Main Campground at Mancos State Park, near the park entrance off County Road N, has twenty-three sites, open year-round. One campsite is designated as wheelchair accessible; RV sites have no hookups. The West Campground, at the north end of Jackson Gulch Reservoir via a park road, has nine tent-only campsites that are not open during the winter. All thirty-two campsites require reservations except during winter (see Appendix A: Resources for details). In the Main Campground, two yurts accommodate up to six people each, available year-round by reservation.

BUREAU OF LAND MANAGEMENT AND DISPERSED CAMPING

There are areas for dispersed camping and BLM camping near the park and monuments. Colorado BLM and Utah BLM both have interactive downloadable maps to help you find campsites. You can also visit a BLM office for information on BLM and dispersed camping (see Appendix A: Resources for details).

WHEN TO VISIT

The park and monuments are open year-round. Autumn brings mild temperatures, fewer crowds, and a variety of colors. Cottonwoods glow with golden hues and Gambel oaks bring a blaze of red to trails. Peak color is typically in early October, but early snow and wind can speed up the process. Although the area is quite beautiful to visit in the winter, services and access to sites are limited in the off-season.

Snowstorms can occur October through May, and though snow accumulations in Mesa Verde have been declining over the past several years, 38 to 112 inches (81 to 284 cm) per year have been recorded. Winter temperatures range from the mid-teens to the upper 30s°F (around 3°C) .

MESA VERDE NATIONAL PARK

Mild temperatures in spring and fall make these the best times to visit Mesa Verde, especially before the increasing heat (temperatures average in the 70s and high 80s Fahrenheit, mid- to high 20s Celsius) and summer crowds. Cliff-dwelling tours begin in mid-May and last through mid-October, weather dependent, and sell out during the peak season, less often in spring and fall. The Spruce Tree

One of the ladders in and out of Square Tower (Trail 8)

House cliff dwelling overlook, Cedar Tree Tower, Chapin Mesa Museum, and the Mesa Top Loop Road are the areas open year-round, weather permitting.

Wetherill Mesa, Morefield Campground, and Far View Lodge are closed in the winter. Park Point, the Far View Sites, and Cliff Palace Loop Road are often closed during winter conditions, but you can snowshoe, cross-country ski, or hike in.

CANYONS OF THE ANCIENTS AND HOVENWEEP NATIONAL MONUMENTS

The best times to visit the monuments are March to late May and September through October when the weather is quite temperate, with lows from 30–50°F (-1–10°C) and highs of 60–80°F (15–27°C). Summer highs can exceed 100°F (38°C), and late-summer monsoons can cause flash floods. Winters are cold: lows average 0–20°F (-18 to -7°C); highs average 30–50°F (-1–10°C). Large snowfalls are uncommon, but even small amounts of snow or ice can make driving difficult.

Winter weather may modify hours at Canyons of the Ancients. The museum has reduced hours and is closed Monday through Wednesday during the peak of winter. Services are also limited in the winter at Hovenweep. The visitor center is closed on Tuesday and Wednesday in the off-season.

PARK AND MONUMENT RULES AND REGULATIONS

Good preparation for your explorations in the Mesa Verde area include an awareness of the managing agencies' rules, regulations, and fees. This section provides important information about what is and is not allowed in the parks and monuments.

FEES

Entry into Mesa Verde National Park requires a day pass, an annual pass for the park, or a National Parks Pass—all entry passes obtained at the park are debit or credit only; no cash is accepted. Tours and permits are an additional cost. There is no fee to visit Canyons of the Ancients National Monument, although there is a charge for visiting the museum. There is no fee to visit Hovenweep National Monument. A visit to Mancos State Park requires a day-use fee or a yearly pass. Touring Hawkins Preserve is free.

PERMITS AND TICKETS

Some of the hikes in Mesa Verde National Park are ranger-guided and ranger-assisted. If Balcony House, Long House, or Cliff Palace are a part of your plans, you must purchase tickets ahead of time to enter these sites. Backcountry tours to Square Tower House, Mug House, and other sites also require

Balcony House (Trail 10) is one of the most well-preserved sites at Mesa Verde National Park.

tickets. Reservations are available online (see Appendix A: Resources for further information). Tickets sell out quickly, so you may need to be flexible with your plans.

Canyons of the Ancients National Monument allows guided tours only by permitted guiding operations. Special permits may be issued for organized group outings. See Appendix A: Contacts for further information.

Signs along the road like this one help you find the trailhead.

DAY-USE AREAS

Several spots along Mesa Verde's main park road feature picnic areas: Mancos Valley Overlook (before Morefield Campground), Montezuma Valley Overlook, Park Point Overlook, and Spruce Tree and Cliff Palace on Chapin Mesa. On Wetherill Mesa Road you can picnic at Window to the Past and at the road's end. During summer at Mesa Verde National Park, sites, picnic areas, and trails are open 8 AM to sunset.

Canyons of the Ancients and Hovenweep National Monuments have small day-use picnic areas at their visitor centers. At Canyons of the Ancients, the following areas are day-use only: the visitor center; Lowry, Painted Hand, and Sand Canyon Pueblos; Upper and Lower Sand Canyon trailheads; and Sand Canyon–Rock Creek Special Recreation Management Area. At Hovenweep, trails are open sunrise to sunset, with only the short overlook trail from the visitor center open after sunset. Picnic tables are located near the visitor center parking lot.

At Hawkins Preserve, the Wyatt picnic area, located between Ruins Road and Hidden Trail not far from Hawkins Pueblo, is a day-use area open during daylight hours when the preserve is open. Mancos State Park has ten picnic tables scattered around the park that are open for use during daylight hours.

BACKCOUNTRY CAMPING

No backcountry camping is permitted in Mesa Verde National Park or Hovenweep National Monument. At Canyons of the Ancients National Monument, camping is allowed only in backcountry areas; no camping is allowed at front-country recreation areas: the Sand Canyon and Rock Creek area, pueblo sites, and all trailheads. No camping permit is needed. Campfires are prohibited in archaeological sites and within 300 feet (91 m) of water sources—ponds, springs, streams—and developed areas including trails, kiosks, and parking areas.

DOGS

Furry friends make great hiking companions. However, dogs are prohibited on most trails at Mesa Verde National Park, with the exception of Long House Loop and the Nordenskiöld Site No. 16 Trail. As with most national parks, dogs are allowed on paved and unpaved roads at Mesa Verde as long as they are leashed. Dogs are also allowed at the Morefield Campground, and up to two pets are allowed at the Far View Lodge with a pet fee. Leashed dogs are allowed on the trails at Canyons of the Ancients and Hovenweep National Monuments, Mancos State Park, and Hawkins Preserve, as well as at any additional trails in this book.

FIREARMS

Using firearms is prohibited in Mesa Verde National Park and Hovenweep National Monument; however, people who can legally possess firearms under applicable federal, state, and local laws may legally possess firearms but must understand and comply with all applicable federal, state, and local firearms laws. Hunting, but not target practice, is allowed only in backcountry areas of Canyons of the Ancients National Monument, as regulated by Colorado Parks and Wildlife. Hunting is prohibited on roads and trails and in campgrounds in Lowry and Sand Canyon Pueblos, in Sand Canyon and Rock Creek Management Area, and in other developed areas.

DRONES

Since 2014, the National Park Service has banned drone operations in all lands under its administration, including national parks, trails, rivers, monuments, and historical parks. Drone usage is also banned at Mancos State Park. However, drone usage is allowed at Hawkins Preserve and other trails mentioned in this book. Please keep in mind that drone usage can disturb visitors and wildlife; see details about other visitors and wildlife in the next section.

WILDLIFE

Feeding, teasing, handling, or capturing wildlife is prohibited in the parks and national monuments. Do not approach animals—including livestock—and leave them undisturbed.

CAMPFIRES

Campfires are permitted only in designated areas when a fire ban is not in place. Do your part to understand the rules and regulations for each area if you are considering building a campfire.

SAFETY AND OUTDOOR ETIQUETTE

It is important to always observe weather conditions when hiking, no matter how short your outing is. Before you head out for your hike, check the forecast. Getting out earlier in the day, especially in summer, decreases the potential for getting caught in a lightning storm. Listen for thunder and watch for increasing clouds as you hike. Get below tree line before early afternoon if lightning threatens.

Take extra precautions if you plan to hike in the evening. The sun sets earlier in the mountains. The sand, rocks, and dirt of mountain or desert trails do not hold their heat, and dry air doesn't hold heat either. Cloudless nights are especially cold. Southwestern Colorado and Southeastern Utah are a desert, so most of the hikes in this book are in dry areas, often in direct sunlight. Avoid long exposure to heat by hiking earlier in the day or choosing routes that contain shade to decrease the risk of overexposure to sunlight and heat.

ENCOUNTERS WITH FLORA AND FAUNA

If you spend enough time in nature, an encounter with a spiky plant or a wild animal is inevitable. Wildlife is more active during dusk and dawn, before and after hibernation, during mating season, and after babies are born. These experiences can be positive and memorable if you remember some essential tips for the animals' safety and your own.

- Wear closed-toed shoes when hiking.
- Check around any rocks or logs before sitting down on them.
- Stay on the trail.
- Pay attention to the trail ahead of you. If you see tracks or scat, notice whether they are fresh or not.
- Although the scenery may be peaceful and quiet, making some noise on the trail—such as low conversation—can reduce the possibility of a surprise encounter.
- Watch wildlife from a distance. Do not try to approach, feed, or follow wildlife.

HAZARDS

Keep your senses aware during your visit to help spot potential hazards or dangerous conditions. Downed trees or branches are hazards you may encounter, as well as others listed below.

Dehydration. Beginning a hike hydrated is a good way to regulate body temperature. The minimum daily need for a day hike is one gallon (four 32-ounce, or one-liter, water bottles). Most of the hikes in this book are shorter than a day hike, but it is never a bad idea to have extra water with you. Early indicators of dehydration include fatigue and lack of urination. Take a break every ten or fifteen minutes and sip water frequently. It is a good rule of thumb to not trust natural water sources that you may find on the trail, no matter how clear the water is. Therefore, it is recommended to carry a hydration pack and a water filter (they are lightweight and inexpensive). It is also recommended that you have additional water in your car for after a hike to keep hydrated.

Altitude sickness. Also known as acute mountain sickness (AMS), altitude sickness can strike anyone despite fitness level or age. Prevent AMS by drinking plenty of fluids and avoiding caffeine and alcohol. Get proper rest before a high-altitude hike. Hike slowly and take frequent breaks. Eat adequately before, during, and after your hike. Altitude sickness can strike from six to twelve hours after being at higher altitudes. The effects of AMS can be felt at elevations as low as 5000 feet (1525 m), but it most often occurs above 8000 feet (2438 m).

AMS symptoms often mimic common symptoms of other conditions. The first and earliest indicator of AMS is a headache. Shortness of breath or rapid breathing, vomiting and/or nausea, fatigue, a lack of appetite, or a lack of urination are some of the most common symptoms. If symptoms do occur, move to a lower elevation. Rest, fluids, and over-the-counter medication should help with any pain. If symptoms persist or worsen, seek medical attention.

Heat exposure, cramps, and exhaustion. Caused by a lack of fluids and electrolytes (mainly salt) in the body, heat exposure's symptoms include dizziness, fatigue, heavy sweating,

The trail to Point Lookout (Hike 3) heads up to an overlook from Morefield Campground.

cold skin, and cramping. To treat, get into the shade. Remove any restrictive clothing and drink liquids every fifteen minutes or so. Apply something cold and massage areas of cramping. If you do not feel improvement after fifteen minutes, seek medical attention.

Heatstroke. When the body temperature exceeds 104°F (40°C), heatstroke occurs. Symptoms are more severe than for heat exposure and heat exhaustion, including dry skin, confusion, erratic behavior, a rapid weak pulse, shallow rapid breathing, and loss of consciousness. Seizures are one of the most severe symptoms. Move to shade and seek medical attention. If possible, remove any tight or sweat-soaked clothing. Drink liquids every minute or so (avoid caffeine or alcohol). Apply something cold to the face, neck, and other areas and ice to the groin, underarms, and wrists.

Hypothermia. Deep snow and patches of ice can be encountered in winter. Hypothermia occurs when the body temperature drops. Common symptoms include shivering, slow shallow breathing, confusion, cold-to-the-touch skin, and a slow weak pulse. If you suspect hypothermia, remove wet clothing. Put on warm dry clothes or wrap in blankets. Drink warm liquids. Move to a warm, dry place and seek medical attention.

Lightning. Both Colorado and Utah are top states for lightning injuries and deaths (number two to avalanches). The highest potential for lightning strikes is between the months of May and August. If you get caught in a storm, find shelter or the lowest spot safe from potential flooding. Stay away from poles, fences, trees, or anything metal. Split apart and keep space between the people in your party. If you feel tingling or your hair standing up, squat low on the balls of your feet and put your head between your legs to make yourself a small target. If you or someone in your party is hit, move to safety as quickly as possible. Call 911 and administer first aid until help arrives.

Flash floods. The most likely places you will see a flash flood are slot canyons, steep slopes, and narrow valleys. The hikes in this book go through canyons and some mini slots and have potential for flash floods. Beyond checking the weather forecast before heading out, check in at visitor centers about the potential for flooding. It is important to understand the difference between a flash flood watch and flash flood warning. A Flash Flood Watch means a flood is possible. A Flash Flood Warning means a flash flood is occurring or will occur soon.

The National Weather Service gives the advice "Turn around, don't drown" for flash floods. It is safer to leave the area of a flash flood than to try to cross it. If a flash flood occurs, seek higher ground immediately, keeping in mind that water levels can exceed 30 feet (9 m) at the flood's strongest.

Steep drop-offs. Some of the hikes in this book have areas of exposure and steep drop-offs. The description of each of these hikes includes information about any exposure and drop-offs.

Rockfall and rock slides. Rock slides are unpredictable and can happen at any time. Some of the hikes in this book travel past scree fields and are on trails susceptible to rockfall. One of the warning signs of a potential rock slide or falling rock is the sound of clapping. If you hear a clapping sound, curl into a ball and protect your head. In addition, the sites in this book are all fragile. When exploring, be cautious due to the potential for rockfall or even site collapses.

Wildfires. The western United States has seen an increase in wildfire activity in the past decade. Recent fires have burned within Mesa Verde National Park, at Hawkins Preserve, and in surrounding areas that may affect trails in this book. Check with each park or monument on the current fire danger risk and for closures due to fire mitigation, cleanup, and restoration. Observe all rules pertaining to campfires, do not discard burning material while hiking or driving, and beware of sparks from a hot car in unpaved areas.

Navigation challenges. Carrying navigation tools (see the Ten Essentials below), knowing your route beforehand, and observing markers while on the trail can help minimize the chance of getting lost. If you do get off the trail or off your route, follow these tips:

1. Stay calm, especially around little children.
2. Stop and view your surroundings.
3. Listen intently for familiar sounds, voices, et cetera off in the distance.
4. Backtrack to your last known point on the trail, or stay where you are. Do not continue forward if you're not sure you can backtrack to the trail.
5. The universal distress signal is a pattern of three: three whistle blows (a whistle carries farther than yelling), three piles of rocks, or three mirror signals. Stop to check whether anyone responds to your signals.
6. If you have cell phone service and none of the above tips help you get back on the right track, contact authorities.

Prickly pear cactus can be found along the trails.

Poisonous flora and cactus spikes. Present on some trails in this guide, poisonous plants can cause some major discomfort if you are exposed to them. Poison ivy and poison hemlock are two of the poisonous flora found on trails in Colorado and Utah; in addition, the milky sap from snow-on-the-mountain can cause contact dermatitis. The best way to avoid poisonous flora is by staying on the trail. Be mindful of hands, arms, legs, and feet when you rest on the side of the trail.

Cactus spikes are also easy to avoid if you stay on the trail. If you come into contact with poisonous plants, wash the area with (preferably warm) water and soap. Apply calamine lotion or baking soda, if available. Call the Poison Control Center (see Appendix A: Resources for details) if you have any questions or concerns.

Bears. Colorado and Utah are home to black bears (which sometimes can be brown in color). Be especially vigilant during dusk and dawn, when they tend to be most active, and in and around campsites you may pass on the trail. If you encounter a bear close to the trail, stop and give it space for an escape route. Do not run. If the bear doesn't retreat after seeing you, pick up small children or position children in between adults. Try to look as large as possible and avoid eye contact. Begin to back up slowly. If attacked, fight back and aim for the nose. Use any objects around you to hit the bear. Do not give up!

Mountain lions. The second largest predator in Colorado and Utah is the mountain lion. Deer are its primary source of food, so be more cautious if you encounter deer on the trail. Mountain lions attack from behind and are most active at dusk and at night. Keeping children in front of the group on the trail is recommended. If you encounter a mountain lion close on the trail, stop and give it space for an escape route. Do not run. Try to look as large as possible and avoid eye contact. Begin to back up slowly. Just as with bears, fight back if you are attacked. Use any objects around you to hit the cougar. Try to protect your head and neck—the spots the lion will most likely aim for. Do not give up!

Other mammals. If you encounter a coyote on the trail, do not run. It will think you are prey trying to escape. Instead, make yourself look bigger, yell, and throw rocks and other items at it to scare it off. Although an attack from elk, moose, or deer is unlikely since they are more apt to run away than charge, it is possible, especially during rut season between late August and October. If you see one of these animals, back away and change the direction you are headed, but do not turn your back. If one charges or attacks, try to get away by placing something large between you and the animal, such as a tree or a car. You may also run, as these types of animals are not likely to chase you. Climbing a tree, rock, or other object is also recommended. If you are attacked, curl up and cover your head. Hold still and wait for the animal to move on.

Snakes. There are three types of venomous snakes in Colorado and seven in Utah—most of the rattlesnake variety. They hibernate in winter; in the heat of the summer, they tend to seek shade, so be especially mindful when taking breaks along the trail. They are most active at dusk and dawn. When the temperature is cooler, snakes will seek warmth from rocks and parts of the trail that receive sun exposure. If possible, walking in the middle of the trail is the safest bet to avoid snakes. If you see one, give it space to escape and warn others around you of the snake's presence. The sound of a rattle means the snake feels threatened and wants you to move away. Back away slowly. If one does come toward you, stomp your foot once and back away quickly.

Spiders and ticks. The desert recluse, black widow, and hobo spiders (often mistaken for a brown recluse) are the most venomous spiders common to the desert and mountains. While most spider bites can be treated with the RICE method—rest, ice, compression, and elevation—be on the lookout for symptoms that mean medical attention needs to be sought: hives, elevated heart rate, rapid breathing, shortness of breath, sweating, cramps, and head and body aches.

The two most prevalent ticks found in Colorado and Utah are the light brown American dog ticks and the dark brown or black wood ticks. Although most common in spring and summer, ticks can be found year-round. Grassy and bushy areas are the most common places ticks are found. Wear tick repellent if you are headed to an area known for ticks. Wearing a long-sleeved shirt and long pants tucked into your socks can also keep ticks from getting onto your skin. After a hike in a tick area, recommended measures to prevent tick-borne diseases are to remove clothing, shower, and carefully remove ticks before they are embedded.

THE TEN ESSENTIALS

The Ten Essentials, originated by The Mountaineers, are items intended to answer two crucial questions: Can you prevent emergencies and respond positively should one occur? And can you safely spend a night—or more—outside? Make sure you pack the following items with you for day hikes.

1. **Navigation.** The five fundamentals are a map, altimeter, compass, GPS device, and personal locator beacon or other device to contact emergency first responders. Do not depend on cell phone service.
2. **Headlamp.** Fully charge yours before you go, or bring extra batteries.
3. **Sun protection.** Wear sunglasses, sun-protective clothes including a hat, sunglasses, and broad-spectrum sunscreen rated at least SPF 30.
4. **First aid.** Carry a basic kit to treat sunburn, cuts and bruises, sprained ankles, and blisters.
5. **Knife.** Also consider a multitool, strong tape, some cordage, and gear-repair supplies.
6. **Fire.** Carry at least one butane lighter (or waterproof matches) and firestarter, such as chemical heat tabs, cotton balls soaked in petroleum jelly, or commercially prepared firestarter.
7. **Shelter.** In addition to a rain shell, carry a single-use bivy sack, plastic tube tent, or jumbo plastic trash bag.
8. **Extra food.** For shorter trips like the hikes covered in this guide, a one-day supply is reasonable.
9. **Extra water.** Carry sufficient water and have the skills and tools required to obtain and purify additional water.
10. **Extra clothes:** Pack additional layers needed to survive the night in the worst conditions that your party may realistically encounter.

Black-and-white pottery was common when the dwellings were inhabited. Admire these artifacts and then leave them where you found them.

OUTDOOR ETIQUETTE

Most of Colorado and Utah is a desert environment, which means that the terrain surrounding the trails in this book is very fragile. To ensure these natural wonders are around for future generations to enjoy, it is important to minimize your impact by observing the following Leave No Trace principles.

Plan ahead and prepare. Know the regulations, check on weather and trail conditions, et cetera.

Travel and camp on durable surfaces. Stay on the designated trails and camp at least 200 feet (61 m) from water. Avoid walking on the delicate desert soil and plants.

Dispose of waste properly. If you must go while on the trail, dig a hole that is 4 to 6 inches (10 to 15 cm) deep at least 200 feet (61 m) away from the trail, campgrounds, and water sources. Bury your waste with dirt and leaves and be sure to pack toilet paper and feminine hygiene products out with you—do not bury them. If you wash hands (and dishes if camping), avoid using soap in a freshwater source. Be sure to pack out all trash and any items you bring with you.

Minimize campfire impacts. If you plan on camping while in the area, be sure to follow all regulations regarding campfires. In such a dry environment, your best bet is to not build campfires at all and to instead use a camp stove.

Respect wildlife. Do not disturb, feed, approach, or handle wildlife.

Be considerate of other visitors. Reduce your noise levels. Leave gates as you found them—opened or closed.

RESPECTING THE SITES

Visiting the Ancestral Puebloan sites in Mesa Verde National Park, Canyons of the Ancients and Hovenweep National Monuments, and the surrounding areas is a walk through time. Your reverence when visiting these sacred places helps ensure that future generations will also be able to enjoy these pieces of important history:

- Pay all necessary permits and entry fees.
- Respect the trail hours. Some of the trails, including those at Hawkins Preserve and Hovenweep National Monument, are open only from sunrise to sunset.
- Listen to the rangers and guides, especially when visiting the sites.
- Stay on the trail. Cryptobiotic soil, vegetation, and outlying areas are fragile.
- Do not remove any artifacts, fossils, or other items you may find on or around the trails and sites. Even if it seems like trash, it may have historical significance. It is illegal to remove anything more than fifty years old.
- Do not touch the walls or the rock art. This can speed up their deterioration.
- Do not enter any structures unless permitted to do so.
- Do not create your own mile markers. While it is tempting to want to create your own cairn, do not disturb the rocks, dirt, and natural environment while on your hike.

SUGGESTED ITINERARIES

These are suggested itineraries for each park or monument based on the number of days you have to visit. Keep in mind that these are just suggestions, and you may not be able to complete everything in the allotted time, depending on travel conditions, park congestion, and other factors.

MESA VERDE NATIONAL PARK

ONE DAY

A single day at Mesa Verde National Park can pack in many highlights and give a big-picture overview of life of the Ancestral Puebloans.

- Mesa Verde National Park Visitor Center
- Far View Sites
- Chapin Mesa Archaeological Museum
- Petroglyph Point hike (Spruce Tree House overlook)
- Guided tour of Cliff Palace, Square Tower House, or Balcony House
- Self-guided tour of Long House on Wetherill Mesa (if you didn't book a guided tour)
- Stargazing

TWO DAYS

With two days in Mesa Verde National Park, you can take both guided and self-guided tours of memorable park highlights, visit several sites, and enjoy dinner at Far View Lodge.

Day One:

- Mesa Verde National Park Visitor Center
- Far View Sites
- Chapin Mesa Archaeological Museum
- Petroglyph Point hike (Spruce Tree House overlook)

- Guided tour of Cliff Palace, Square Tower House, or Balcony House
- Self-guided tour of Long House on Wetherill Mesa (if you didn't book a guided tour)
- Stargazing

Day Two:
- Self-guided tour of Long House on Wetherill Mesa
- Mesa Top Loop Road drive (stop at overlooks)
- Soda Canyon Trail hike
- Knife Edge Trail hike
- Dinner at Far View Lodge
- Evening program at Morefield Campground amphitheater

THREE DAYS

Three days in the park allows you time to get to know the Mesa Verde region. From guided and self-guided tours to the geology of the area, this itinerary allows visitors to enjoy the full park experience.

Day One:
- Mesa Verde National Park Visitor Center
- Far View Sites
- Chapin Mesa Archaeological Museum
- Petroglyph Point hike (Spruce Tree House overlook)
- Guided tour of Cliff Palace, Square Tower House, or Balcony House
- Self-guided tour of Long House at Wetherill Mesa (if you didn't book a guided tour)
- Stargazing

Day Two:
- Self-guided tour of Long House at Wetherill Mesa (if you didn't book a guided tour)

- Mesa Top Loop Road drive (stop at overlooks)
- Soda Canyon Trail hike
- Knife Edge Trail hike
- Dinner at Far View Lodge
- Evening program at Morefield Campground amphitheater

Day Three:

- Spruce Canyon Trail hike
- Guided tour of Cliff Palace, Square Tower House, or Balcony House
- Farming Terrace Trail hike
- Point Lookout Trail hike
- Prater Ridge Trail hike (if looking for some miles)

CANYONS OF THE ANCIENTS NATIONAL MONUMENT

ONE DAY

A one-day visit to Canyons of the Ancients National Monument gives you a sneak peek at the highest known archaeological site density in the United States.

- Canyons of the Ancients Visitor Center and Museum
- Lowry Pueblo
- Painted Hand Pueblo
- Sand Canyon hike (hike early before it gets too warm)

TWO DAYS

Since Canyon of the Ancients National Monument is so spread out, two days within the monument gives you a big picture view of the lives of the Ancestral Puebloans.

Day One:

- Canyons of the Ancients Visitor Center and Museum

- Lowry Pueblo
- Painted Hand Pueblo
- Sand Canyon (hike early before it gets too warm)

Day Two:

- East Rock Creek Trail

HOVENWEEP NATIONAL MONUMENT

ONE DAY

A one-day trip to Hovenweep, with some driving, provides an overlook of the towers built by the Ancestral Puebloans between CE 1200 and 1300.

- Hovenweep National Monument visitor center
- Square Tower Group
- Horseshoe and Hackberry Trails
- Holly Tower Group hike

TWO DAYS

Spending two days at Hovenweep National Monument allows visitors to get an up-close look at the structures built in the area from CE 1200 to 1300 by the Ancestral Puebloans.

Day One:

- Hovenweep National Monument visitor center
- Square Tower Group
- Horseshoe and Hackberry Trails
- Stargazing

Day Two:

- Holly Tower Group hike

HOW TO USE THIS GUIDE

The hikes in this book range from desert to alpine, highlighting the best of the varied terrain of Mesa Verde National Park, nearby national monuments, and the Cortez area. These hikes are just a sample of the beauty of Southwestern Colorado.

This guide breaks down this vast region into four parts: Mesa Verde National Park, Canyons of the Ancients and Hovenweep National Monuments, and the three towns around which these entities are located. Three of these four parts are broken down into chapters based on geographic centers for hikes and services. These chapters include a brief overview of the features you can expect to find and a summary of services.

Each trail description includes information about the route, notes about the particular hike, directions to the trailhead using car transportation, how to follow the given route, and ways to extend the hike (when applicable).

All distances, elevation gains, and high points were derived using GPS data from Gaia GPS and Caltopo (see Appendix A: Resources for details). The information is presented in the English system (feet and miles) as well as the metric system (meters and kilometers). Mileage shown for each hike is roundtrip. Research routes ahead of your trip, and download maps of the hikes ahead of time (or carry a topo map) to be sure you can navigate any hike safely.

OPPOSITE: *Mancos Shale is found along the mesa in Montezuma Valley.*

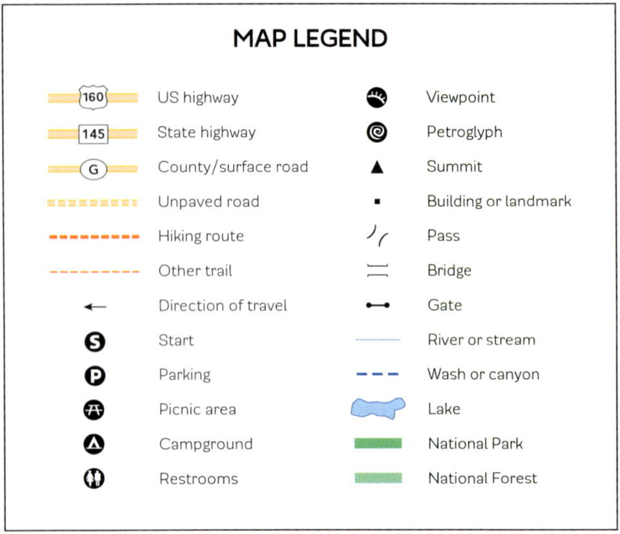

There are three levels of trail difficulty: easy, moderate, and challenging. The ratings are created with the average hiker in mind—someone with a general level of experience and fitness. The difficulty rating is based on mileage and elevation gain. Several factors including terrain and trail surface may also affect the rating.

Easy: These are short, more family-friendly hikes that most hikers can complete with little difficulty; distances are 0.3 mile to 3 miles (0.4 to 5 km) with 300 feet (9 m) of elevation gain or less.

Moderate: These longer or more difficult hikes of a distance of 1 mile (1.6 km) or more can be completed in one to three hours by experienced hikers; there may be up to 500 feet (152 m) of elevation gain and the route may include ladders.

Challenging: These half-day to one-day hikes for experienced hikers may include some scrambling, steep drop-offs, and ladders.

The Map section references the Trails Illustrated topographic map for the area for routefinding. Caltopo and Gaia GPS are superb resources for customizing maps for your specific hike (see Appendix A: Resources for details). Since some of these hikes include desert travel through washes, it is a good idea to carry a topographic map and compass for routefinding. In addition, each hike includes a trail map, and some chapters and regions also feature an area map to help you locate hikes in some of the more far-flung or remote places.

GPS coordinates show the location of each trailhead based on WGS 84 datum. They are listed in decimal degree form, the easiest one to put into applications like Google Maps.

The Notes section includes information specific to each hike, including whether .dogs are allowed, restroom and water access, permits, terrain and navigation, interpretive features, and the like.

Use the Getting There section for directions to each trailhead from either the park entrance or visitor center—or in

A NOTE ABOUT SAFETY

Safety is an important concern in all outdoor activities. No guidebook can alert you to every hazard or anticipate the limitations of every reader. Therefore, the descriptions of roads, trails, routes, and natural features in this book are not representations that a particular place or excursion will be safe for your party. When you follow any of the routes described in this book, you assume responsibility for your own safety. Under normal conditions, such excursions require the usual attention to traffic, road and trail conditions, weather, terrain, the capabilities of your party, and other factors. Keeping informed on current conditions and exercising common sense are the keys to a safe, enjoyable outing.

—*Mountaineers Books*

some cases the nearest town. Mesa Verde National Park and Hovenweep National Monument have only one entrance, while directions for Canyons of the Ancients National Monument are given from both the visitor center for northern sites and from Cortez, the nearest town to the southern sites.

A summary of each hike highlights noteworthy features. The On the Trail section contains point A to point B directions for navigating each hike safely. Use the Going Farther section to extend a hike when possible or to look for alternative routes back to the trailhead.

OPPOSITE: *Wooden beams continue to hold up the Balcony House (Hike 10).*

PART 1: MESA VERDE NATIONAL PARK

OVERVIEW OF MESA VERDE NATIONAL PARK
To 145
184
Mancos
160
To Cortez
To Durango
160
Morefield Village
1–3
Mesa Verde Visitor and Research Center
Far View Lodge
Mesa Top Ruins Rd
MESA VERDE NATIONAL PARK
Wetherill Mesa Rd
Mesa Top Ruins Rd
4
5
Farming Terrace
12
Chapin Mesa Archaeological Museum
6–7
13
14
Cliff Palace Loop
8
9–11
Mesa Top Loop
N
0
5 miles
0
5 kms

MOREFIELD VILLAGE

The first area of Mesa Verde National Park found south of the entrance station is Morefield Village, where the park's campground is located. Here you'll also find a ranger station, camper store, cafe, and gas station. Trailers and towed vehicles are prohibited beyond Morefield, so if you're not camping here, there is a parking area between the highway and the park entrance station for leaving towed trailers or vehicles.

1 PRATER RIDGE LOOP

Distance: 7.8 miles (19 km)
Elevation gain: 675 feet (205 m)
High point: 8422 feet (2567 m)
Difficulty: Challenging
Trail surface: Dirt, slickrock, logs
Map: Trails Illustrated Mesa Verde
GPS: 37.29667°N, 108.41819°W
Notes: Dogs prohibited; restrooms at campground and Morefield Village; water access at Morefield Village

> The highlight of the Prater Ridge Trail is the viewpoints, but the downside is that it is mostly exposed, with only pockets of shade—bring plenty of water and a hat. In the summer when the chance of afternoon thunderstorms is high, start early, as there is no place to seek shelter on the ridge. The

The North Loop overlooks the Morefield Campground.

trail is open to hikers and snowshoers in the winter—snowshoes are required when the Morefield loops are groomed.

GETTING THERE

From the town of Cortez, head east on US 160 for almost 10 miles (16 km). Take the exit toward Mesa Verde National Park and turn right onto Mesa Top Ruins Road, the main park road. Head south for 3.9 miles (6.3 km), then turn right at the Morefield Campground sign, and in a short distance park at the trailhead on the left.

ON THE TRAIL

Beginning from the southwest side of Morefield Campground, the trail gains elevation from the get-go, so your legs will warm up quickly. At a little over 0.2 mile (0.3 km), keep left at the junction with the connector that heads to the Knife Edge Trail (Hike 2). As you climb, you'll have views of Morefield Campground below and Lone Cone and Point Lookout in the distance.

Along the trail, watch for mule deer, bears, and wild turkeys. Collared lizards and utas (side-blotched lizards in the genus *Uta*) sun on the rocks. Sego lilies, as well as Mesa

Verde cactus, musk thistle, and multiple colors of prickly pear cactus, line the trail.

Just shy of 0.6 mile (0.9 km), the trail bends, leaving the campground views behind and heading south while continuing to climb among sagebrush and mossy rocks. In the summer, abundant wildflowers line the trail, drawing a buzz of activity from bees to hummingbirds.

At a switchback at 0.7 mile (1.1 km), look right for views of Sleeping Ute Mountain. Now high above Montezuma Valley, you'll see the San Juan Mountains come into view. After a little more climbing, the trail flattens out to a wide open area that is often filled with birdsong and soaring butterflies. There are many spots on the left to take in views of the city of Mancos as you watch western tanagers flit about.

At just over 1 mile (1.6 km), turn right at a junction with a short connector trail to head onto the north loop. Prater Ridge, named for a pioneer family who built a homestead in Prater Canyon, separates Prater Canyon and Morefield Canyon and offers extensive viewpoints in several directions as

PARK POINT OVERLOOK

Not to be confused with the Point Lookout Trail (Hike 3), the Park Point Overlook is worth a stop off Mesa Top Ruins Road. Located on the north side of the road about 11 miles (17 km) from the park entrance, this paved trail takes you 0.2 mile (0.3 km) to the park's highest point, with some of the best views in the park. Look north to see the San Juan Mountains or south into New Mexico on clear days. The overlook is a great place to have a picnic.

About halfway along this short trail, you can also walk about 0.1 mile (0.2 km) to the Park Point Fire Lookout, built in the 1930s and used by the park during fire season for communication about weather, active fires, and lightning within the park and surrounding areas.

The terrain of the Praeter Ridge Trail varies between scrubrush and pines.

you hike. The path opens up a bit a little past 1.9 miles (3 km), but stay left to follow the obvious trail. Here you begin to see evidence of the 1996 Chapin No. 5 Fire and the 2000 Bircher Fire that burned along both loops of the trail.

The trail begins to get rocky around 2.3 miles (3.7 km). Soon you come upon a great place for a water and snack break with western views. Look for cairns to guide you. Just past 4.2 miles (6.8 km) is a sign for the connector trail on the left that returns to the campground; continue straight to begin the south loop.

At around 4.4 miles (7 km), the vegetation thickens and trees are more abundant—both new postfire growth and those that survived the blaze. The smell of pine is strong in this area. The trail opens up more, allowing views of the walls of Prater Canyon. Can you picture where a family might create a homestead in the area?

As the trail begins to turn eastward, you get glimpses of the park road. At 5.4 miles (8.7 km), look right to see Morefield Campground and the starting point for this hike. Past the 6-mile (9.7 km) mark, the trail reaches the first junction

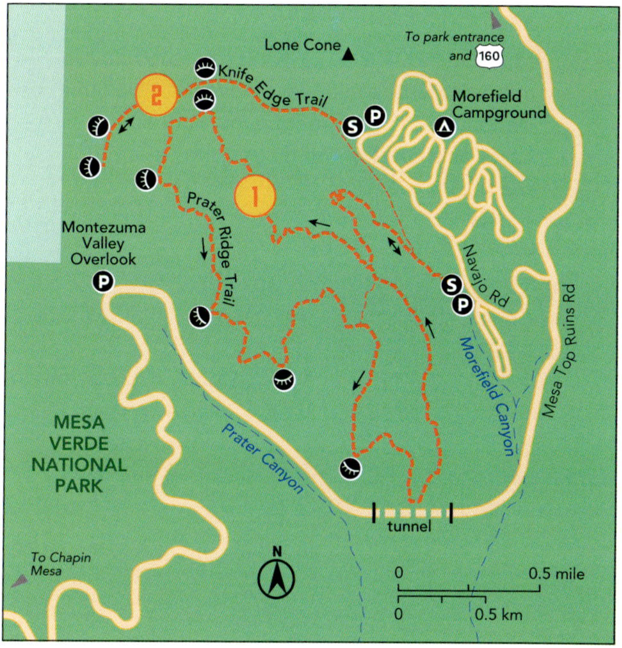

with the connector trail. Continue right to stay on the south loop, which very shortly meets up with the north loop and the trail leading back to the trailhead at 6.3 miles (10 km). Veer right here to retrace your steps to the trailhead.

2 KNIFE EDGE

Distance: 2 miles (3.2 km)
Elevation gain: 62 feet (18 m)
High point: 7800 feet (2380 m)
Difficulty: Easy
Trail surface: Dirt, gravel
Map: Trails Illustrated Mesa Verde

The trail has great views as it follows the bluff.

GPS: 38.6026965°N, 109.3432778°W

Notes: Dogs prohibited; restrooms in campground and Morefield Village; water access at Morefield Village

> This interpretive trail takes you along part of the original main park road. Following the old roadbed and a knife-edge bluff, it is nevertheless great for kids and boasts some of the most beautiful views of the surrounding mountains in Montezuma Valley and thirty-two types of plants and wildflowers. Hike this trail at sunset for color cascading behind the mountains. You may snowshoe this trail in winter. (See Hike 2 map.)

GETTING THERE

From the town of Cortez, head east on US 160 for almost 10 miles (16 km). Take the exit toward Mesa Verde National Park and turn right onto Mesa Top Ruins Road, the main park road. Head south for 3.9 miles (6.3 km), then turn right at the Morefield Campground sign, traveling 0.6 mile (0.9 km) and continuing onto Navajo Road, which turns into Hopi Road. Follow this for 0.4 mile (0.6 km). The trailhead and parking lot are on the left.

ON THE TRAIL

From the parking lot, look for the trail sign to find the beginning of this dirt and gravel trail. If there are trail brochures, grab one to help in identifying plants and wildflowers including larkspur, wild tarragon, and snowberry.

The trail climbs slightly through a meadow on the east side of Prater Ridge, then through piñon pine and Gambel oak before intersecting with a connector to the Prater Ridge Trail (Hike 1) to the left at about 0.1 mile (0.2 km). Head straight as you continue to climb. Two tall rock features made of Point Lookout Sandstone hugging you in were once said to scare

HUMMINGBIRD STUDY

Since 2007, Mesa Verde National Park has been part of the Hummingbird Monitoring Network (HMN), which studies the migratory routes and habits of hummingbirds throughout the national parks. Through the North American Bird Banding Program (NABBP), volunteers study population numbers, diversity, and more at monitoring sites. You can volunteer to be a part of citizen science and help this migratory population while visiting the park. Opportunities to help band hummingbirds within the park occur in August. Contact the HMN or Mesa Verde National Park for more information (see Appendix A: Resources).

Views of Sleeping Ute Mountain and the La Sal Mountains are found at the trail's end.

motorists who worried about the stability of these rocks as they traveled the park road. The trail opens up at nearly 0.25 mile (0.4 km) for amazing views on the right-hand side.

Birds and white admiral butterflies enjoy serviceberries and chokecherries all along the trail edges. At a little more than 0.5 mile (0.8 km), views of Mancos Shale and Point Lookout Sandstone can be seen on the right-hand side. Once this was the Western Interior Seaway, and as the sea advanced westward it left deposits of the gray Mancos Shale you see today. On top of the Mancos Shale is the Point Lookout Formation. As seen from the park entrance and along the Knife Edge Trail, this formation is made of buff and tan sandstone formed before the seaway finally retreated.

Rusted metal and pipes along the trail were once part of the original park system. See if you can spot the pink tubular flowers of Hayden's gilia (*Aliciella haydenii*) or the bright yellow flowers of *Mentzelia multiflora*, two rare species of wildflower seen along the Knife Edge Trail.

The trail dead-ends at 1 mile (1.6 km) at a viewpoint looking across Montezuma Valley. A sign stating "Stop! Trail End!

Slide Area" tells you that you have reached the trail's end. Before returning the way you came, enjoy vistas of Sleeping Ute Mountain in the distance as well as the San Miguel and Abajo Mountains on a clear day. The La Plata Mountains seen along the trail and Sleeping Ute Mountain are laccolithic intrusions, created by magma pushing layers of rock above to create a mushroom or dome shape.

I once encountered a western king snake on this trail—a good reminder about the numerous species found in the park and the need to be vigilant and stay on the trail, especially since rattlesnakes inhabit the area. Bears, mule deer, bobcats, and bald eagles are also common in Mesa Verde, so keep your eyes open and you may spot some interesting wildlife.

3 POINT LOOKOUT

Distance: 2.2 miles (3.5 km)
Elevation gain: 400 feet (121 m)
High point: 8427 feet (2568 m)
Difficulty: Moderate
Trail surface: Dirt, slickrock, logs
Map: Trails Illustrated Mesa Verde
GPS: 37.3071471°N, 108.4226587°W
Note: Dogs prohibited; restrooms at campground and Morefield Village; water access at Morefield Village

> The Point Lookout Trail doesn't highlight sites or archaeological history, but it provides some of the best views, from one of the park's highest points. The trail is steep and rocky, with thirty switchbacks; some hikers may want hiking poles. There is little to no shade; bring water and a hat. This hike is best May through October but is open to hikers or snowshoers in winter—snowshoes are required when the Morefield loops are groomed.

GETTING THERE

From the town of Cortez, head east on US 160 for almost 10 miles (16 km). Take the exit toward Mesa Verde National Park and turn right onto Mesa Top Ruins Road, the main park road. Head south for 3.9 miles (6.3 km), then turn right at the Morefield Campground sign, continuing onto Navajo Road, which turns into Hopi Road. Follow this for 1.6 miles (2.6 km) to the end of the road at amphitheater parking and the trailhead.

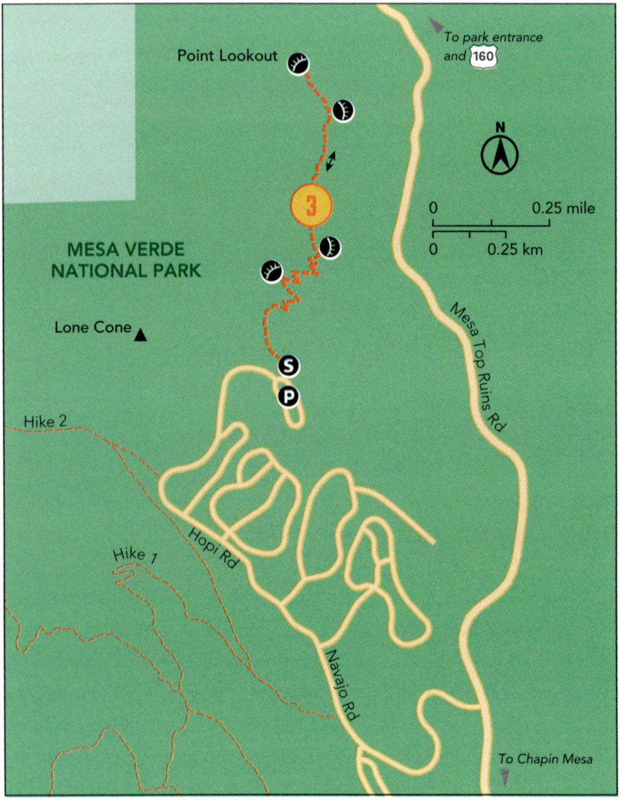

The Point Lookout Trail offers several viewpoints of the surrounding area.

ON THE TRAIL

Beginning from the amphitheater area at Morefield Campground, this hike is especially good in early morning or at sunset when there is more abundant shade. The trail starts surrounded by areas of brush—Mesa Verde deer are common here around the trail. Mormon tea, yucca, and Indian paintbrush line the trail in full bloom from spring to fall. At a bit more than 0.1 mile (0.2 km), the trail bends right and the first of many switchbacks begin.

This trail climbs slowly and steadily through Morefield Canyon, switchbacking up to the top to 360-degree views, including the La Plata and San Juan Mountains and Mancos and Montezuma Valleys. As you climb, you will ascend steps made of rocks and logs. Piñon pines line the trail. The views begin almost immediately.

At about 0.25 mile (0.4 km), rocks provide a place to take a quick drink. The exposed area offers basking spots for lizards, frequently seen along the trail. A view of the Knife Edge of the park comes into view. This was once part of the Western Interior Seaway; as the sea advanced westward it

Hikers will enjoy the expansive vista to the west of Point Lookout.

left deposits of the gray Mancos Shale you see today. Over the Mancos Shale is the buff or tan Point Lookout Formation of sandstone formed before the seaway finally retreated.

When you reach about 0.4 mile (0.7 km), there are larger slabs of rock to walk across and climb up. You won't see many trail signs, but getting lost is impossible. Be sure to stay on the trail, as rattlesnake sightings are common.

Butterflies and bees float past you as they grab pollen and nectar from abundant cactus and a variety of wildflowers including mule's ears and penstemon that showcase their color spring through fall. The trail begins to level off for a break at about 0.6 mile (1 km). Offshoots on the right provide views of the San Juan and La Plata Mountains as the trail crosses the mesa top.

Panoramic views begin at 0.9 mile (1.5 km) with several overlooks. The trail steps down at 1 mile (1.6 km) with views

all around. Tell everyone that you have been to the top of the geological formation that represents Mesa Verde National Park when seen from outside the park. Look for the park road and visitor and research center to the northeast, along with Mancos Shale, Point Lookout Formation, and the Knife Edge Trail (Hike 2) to the west.

Sleeping Ute Mountain is in the distance taking his daily nap. The La Plata Mountains viewed along the trail and Sleeping Ute are laccolithic intrusions, created by magma pushing layers of rock above to create mushroom or dome shapes.

There isn't another hike within the park that offers such an iconic view of Southwestern Colorado than this one, so don't rush to leave. After drinking in the views, turn around and head back down the switchbacks. Don't forget to stop and enjoy the views as you return to the trailhead.

MESA TOP RUINS ROAD

South beyond Morefield Village, Mesa Top Ruins Road passes through the Morefield-Prater tunnel and in about 2.5 miles (4 km) reaches the turnoff to the Montezuma Valley Overlook, with restrooms and picnic tables. As the road traverses the North Rim, in another 3.5 miles (5.6 km) or so is a turnoff on the right for the drive and short hike to Park Point. In another 2.5 miles (4 km) or so, a turnoff is on the right for Geologic Overlook, with restrooms. The park road reaches the Far View area in about 2.5 more miles (4 km), with a cafe, gift shop, and lodge overlooking Soda Canyon; shortly beyond is the turn for the Wetherill Mesa Road. To reach this chapter's hikes, continue south on Mesa Top Ruins Road toward Chapin Mesa.

FAR VIEW VISITOR CENTER

Opened in 1967, the Far View Visitor Center is located essentially in the center of the park. With wraparound views and a shape similar to a kiva, it was one of the very first visitor centers to open in the national park system and was designed by Colorado architects Joseph and Louise Marlow with the input of the National Park Service Western Office of Design and Construction. In 2013, it was replaced by a much larger visitor center near the park entrance.

In 2023, the nonprofit Colorado Preservation added the Far View Visitor Center to its annual list of Colorado's Most

OPPOSITE: *Rock art can be found at Pipe Shrine House (Hike 4).*

Endangered Places. Due to the building's condition, most proposals—including a museum and education center—have not had traction. As of this writing, the Far View Visitor Center remains closed.

4 FAR VIEW SITES

Distance: 1 mile (1.6 km)
Elevation gain: 185 feet (56 m)
High point: 7750 feet (2362 m)
Difficulty: Easy
Trail surface: Pavement, dirt, slickrock
Map: Trails Illustrated Mesa Verde
GPS: 37.2393735°N, 108.5042854°W
Note: Dogs prohibited; seasonal portable toilets (not wheelchair-accessible); no water access

> This densely populated farming community was occupied from CE 800 to 1300; more than twenty sites remain, but only six have been excavated. The interpretive sites provide literature at viewpoints; viewing times are 8 AM to sunset. This is a shadier hike, but a hat and water are still recommended. A seasonal volunteer or ranger may be present to answer questions. This trail is best hiked May through October. Due to resource damage, this trail may be closed in winter.

GETTING THERE

From the town of Cortez, head east on US 160 for almost 10 miles (16 km). Take the exit toward Mesa Verde National Park and turn right onto Mesa Top Ruins Road, the main park road. Follow the road south for 16.4 miles (26.4 km). Turn left at the sign for Far View Sites and drive the road about 200 yards (182 m) to the trailhead.

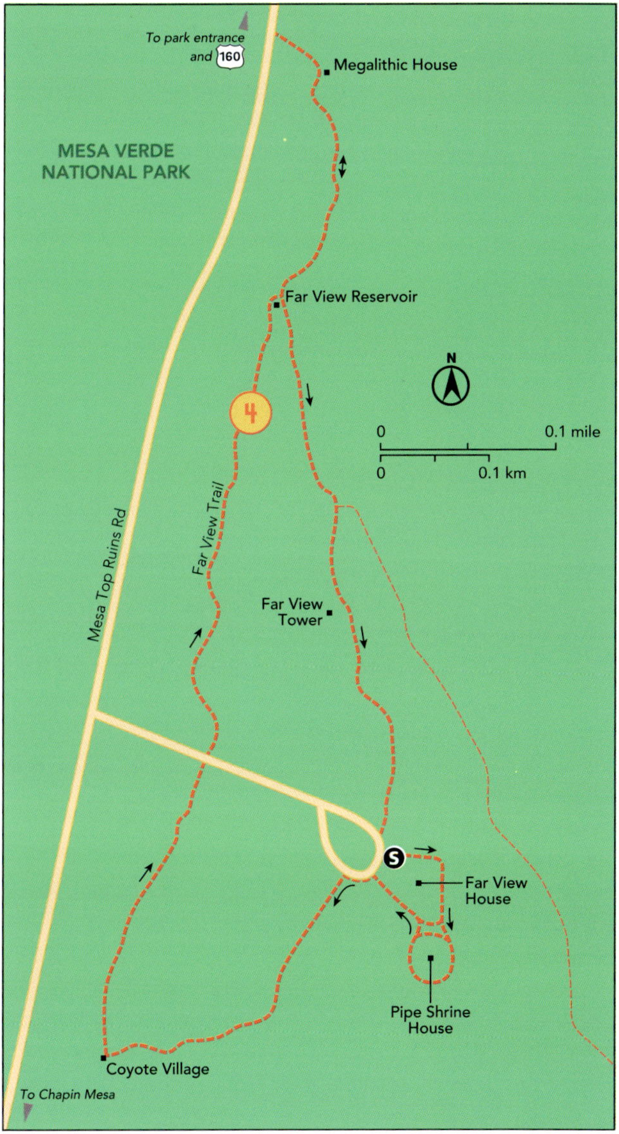
To park entrance
and 160
Megalithic House
MESA VERDE
NATIONAL PARK
Far View Reservoir
N
4
0
0.1 mile
0
0.1 km
Far View Trail
Mesa Top Ruins Rd
Far View
Tower
S
Far View
House
Pipe Shrine
House
Coyote Village
To Chapin Mesa

You can view a kiva in Pipe Shrine House.

ON THE TRAIL

Nearly fifty villages have been identified within a half square mile (1.3 sq km) area at the Far View Sites, home to hundreds of people in what was a densely populated area. The sites reveal evidence of families that chose to stay on the mesa top instead of living in the alcoves elsewhere in the park. These Ancient Puebloans grew the three sisters—corn, beans, and squash—to feed their families and community.

At one time, a dirt road directly connected the structures and visitors were allowed to climb on the sites. Looting and destruction caused the park to close the road and restrict climbing. There are two ways you can hike the trail: This hike heads clockwise, with the last structure to see being the Far View Tower. (You can also hike counterclockwise and begin with the tower after viewing Far View House.)

From the trailhead, begin with a tour around the Far View House, an example of a "Great House": geometrically formed with thirty-plus rooms and a large kiva, with three small kivas added later.

Behind the Far View House, follow the signs south (left) to the Pipe Shrine House. Explore the house and kiva from a distance, as you are not allowed to enter the site. Can you find the spiral stone? What do you think the significance of the spiral is?

From the Pipe Shrine House, continue clockwise on the loop, back to the parking lot, and look for signs for the Far View Trail; head southwest on this paved trail to Coyote Village. The typical wildflowers and cactus found throughout the park grow in abundance here.

Coyote Village appears at around 0.3 mile (0.5 km). Visitors are free to explore the village, but do not climb the walls. Oils on hands can leave marks and damage the masonry, so take caution to not touch the stones. The village has some of the highest concentration of artifacts found within the park, especially pottery, helping to date when the village was inhabited. Do not take any artifacts you may find around the village. Consider mentioning what you find to a ranger, to be sure it is properly preserved.

From Coyote Village, head north on the flat trail. Be careful where the trail crosses the service road to the parking lot. Beyond the village the trail passes among shady pines toward the Far View Reservoir. You may see a Mesa Verde deer if you visit in the morning or evening. Lizards are often sunning themselves on the structures.

Coming into view at about 0.5 mile (0.8 km) is the Far View Reservoir. Now dry, this served as a prominent water source for the complex of farms and homes along the mesa top. The white plastic pipes (known as piezometers) in the reservoir were installed in the 1990s to monitor groundwater in the reservoir. It has been found that much of the water that was collected in the reservoir came from snowmelt and storm runoff.

Take a detour off the main trail and head left (north) to the Megalithic House, at about 0.7 mile (1.1 km). This extremely vulnerable structure, now protected from rain and snow, is one of the few single-family dwellings in this area. Why would this family have lived away from the larger community on their own? With land and easy access to the reservoir, it would have been easy to be self-sufficient to grow food. Warmer nights on the mesa than in the canyons would have meant better potential crop growth. You may also notice edible plants all around the trail, from Mormon tea to cattails, which were used for making medicine, baskets, and more.

Backtrack to the main trail and continue south. At a trail junction at about 0.8 mile (1.3 km), stay right to reach Far View Tower in about 200 yards (183 m). Towers were used for safety, from spotting fire and incoming weather to providing protection from other tribes. In the 1920s, concrete was used to hastily improve the structural integrity of the tower. Recent work has been done to replace the concrete with mortar to help with weathering.

After visiting the tower, continue south on the trail for another 0.1 mile (0.2 km) to return to the trailhead. Which site was your favorite on the trail? Do you have any questions the volunteer or ranger could answer?

5 FARMING TERRACE

Distance: 0.5 mile (0.8 km)
Elevation gain: 75 feet (22 m)
High point: 7108 feet (2166 m)
Difficulty: Easy
Trail surface: Dirt, stone stairs
Map: Trails Illustrated Mesa Verde
GPS: 37.1973591°N, 108.4852942°W
Note: Dogs prohibited; no restrooms or water access

The short Farming Terrace Trail offers a different perspective on the life of the Ancestral Puebloans. The rock terraces were check dams that helped with erosion and water retention on dryland farming. The area is still recovering from the 2002 Long Mesa Fire that burned the titular juniper tree once standing near the Cedar Tree Tower and kiva. There is no shade here, so fill up your water container. This hike is best May through October.

GETTING THERE

From the town of Cortez, head east on US 160 for almost 10 miles (16 km). Take the exit toward Mesa Verde National

On the Farming Terrace Trail, you can find the remnants of check dams used for dry farming.

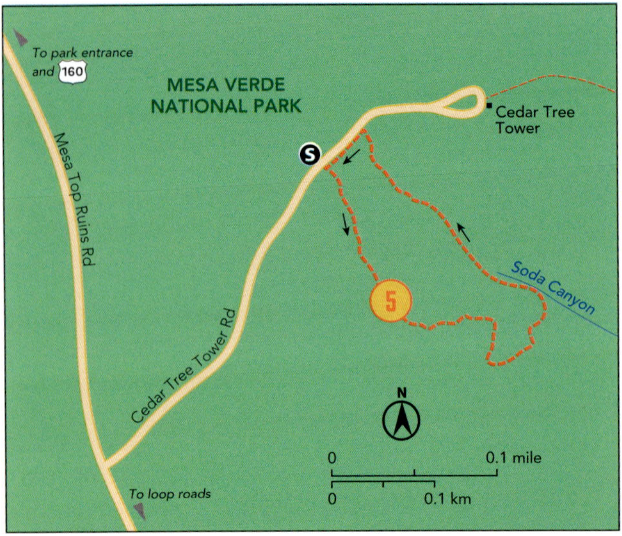

Park and turn right onto Mesa Top Ruins Road, the main park road. Follow the road south for 19.6 miles (31.5 km). Turn left at the sign for Cedar Tree Tower Road and in 0.2 mile (0.3 km), the trailhead is on the right.

ON THE TRAIL

This short hike begins on a dirt path along the mesa top. Burned trees are evidence of the Long Mesa Fire. Large rocks along the trail likely represent where check dams were once in place but have eroded away over time.

The trail begins to descend into the drainage of Soda Canyon headed southeast. At about 0.1 mile (0.2 km), rock stairs take you down into the drainage. Be on the lookout for lizards, including the sagebrush swift and rock swift—both common in the surrounding terrain along this trail. Rufous hummingbirds are also common in the warmer months.

At 0.2 mile (0.3 km), a section of check dams has been preserved by the park service. The interpretive signage tells

Cedar Tree Tower is a short distance from the Farming Terrace Trail.

what purpose the dams served in crop production for the Ancestral Puebloans. Another sign details information about soil and water conservation.

Through the wash in Soda Canyon, the trail bends and begins to climb again at 0.25 mile (0.4 km), now leading northwest. Continue to look for evidence of check dams while picturing the hardships of dryland farming with only the tools the land provides, including rocks.

Once back at Cedar Tree Tower Road, follow the road northeast less than 0.1 mile (0.2 km) to Cedar Tree Tower and kiva. Spend some time observing the tower and kiva from a distance, guessing what the structures were used for. How the tower was used is a mystery, but there is speculation that it played a part in ceremonies or was a lookout tower to keep crops safe. Retrace your steps back along the road a little over 0.1 mile (0.2 km) to the trailhead.

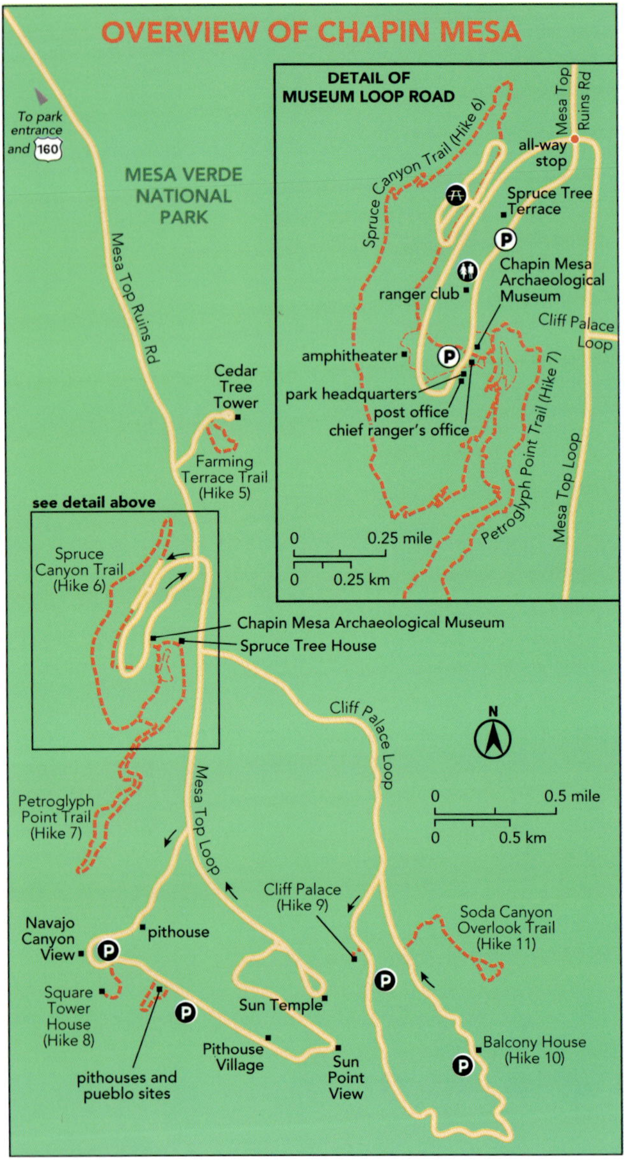

OVERVIEW OF CHAPIN MESA
To park entrance and 160
MESA VERDE NATIONAL PARK
Mesa Top Ruins Rd
Cedar Tree Tower
Farming Terrace Trail (Hike 5)
see detail above
Spruce Canyon Trail (Hike 6)
Chapin Mesa Archaeological Museum
Spruce Tree House
Cliff Palace Loop
Mesa Top Loop
Petroglyph Point Trail (Hike 7)
0 0.5 mile
0 0.5 km
N
Navajo Canyon View
pithouse
Square Tower House (Hike 8)
pithouses and pueblo sites
Sun Temple
Pithouse Village
Sun Point View
Cliff Palace (Hike 9)
Soda Canyon Overlook Trail (Hike 11)
Balcony House (Hike 10)
DETAIL OF MUSEUM LOOP ROAD
Spruce Canyon Trail (Hike 6)
Mesa Top Ruins Rd
all-way stop
Spruce Tree Terrace
Chapin Mesa Archaeological Museum
ranger club
Cliff Palace Loop
amphitheater
park headquarters
post office
chief ranger's office
Petroglyph Point Trail (Hike 7)
Mesa Top Loop
0 0.25 mile
0 0.25 km

CHAPIN MESA

Mesa Top Ruins Road continues south to Chapin Mesa, the location of Mesa Verde National Park headquarters. At the all-way stop, the road to the right takes you to the Spruce Canyon area, where you'll find the Chapin Mesa Archaeological Museum, a cafe and gift shop, a picnic area, an amphitheater, and two popular trails. Enjoy some time at the museum galleries, showcasing sandals, pottery, and more artifacts found within the park. Spruce Tree House, once reachable on a self-guided trail, is currently closed for safety.

From the all-way stop, the Mesa Tops Ruins Road heading south soon reaches a Y intersection. To the right is the Mesa Top Loop road to Square Tower House (a guided-tour reservation is required); to the left is the Cliff Palace Loop road to Cliff Palace and Balcony House (tickets are required to tour these sites). The Cliff Palace Loop road follows above Soda Canyon, whose name is derived from the white calcium-carbonate deposits you can see below the rim. Along both loop roads are viewpoints and restrooms; the Cliff Palace Loop road also has a picnic area.

6 SPRUCE CANYON LOOP

Distance: 2.4 miles (3.9 km)
Elevation gain: 558 feet (170 m)
High point: 8427 feet (2166 m)
Difficulty: Moderate

Trail surface: Dirt, slickrock, roots, steps
Map: Trails Illustrated Mesa Verde
GPS: 38.592236°N, 109.3838341°W
Note: Dogs prohibited; restrooms, water access in parking area and museum

> The Spruce Canyon Trail takes you through all four of the park's ecosystems: shrub-steppe, piñon-juniper woodland, mountain shrub, and Douglas-fir–ponderosa pine woodland. A bit shadier than most hikes in the park, this trail is best May through October. The trail is open for hiking and snowshoeing in the winter if conditions permit. Combine it with the Petroglyph Point Trail (Hike 7) for a loop of 4.8 miles (7.8 km).

GETTING THERE

From the town of Cortez, head east on US 160 for almost 10 miles (16 km). Take the exit toward Mesa Verde National Park and turn right onto Mesa Top Ruins Road, the main park road. Follow it south for 20 miles (32 km) to the all-way stop. Turn right and follow this one-way loop road for 0.7 mile (1.1 km) to the parking area near Chapin Mesa Archaeological Museum.

ON THE TRAIL

This trail can be hiked in either direction. This description heads clockwise beginning with the descent into Spruce Canyon. Sign in at the museum registry, and then follow signs for the Spruce Tree House along the paved path into the canyon. You will likely hear birds singing, and butterflies love the abundant flowering cacti and other plants. Lizards and squirrels scurry in the underbrush—a little noise in a very quiet environment.

At a little over 0.1 mile (0.2 km), you pass the side trail on the left to Spruce Tree House, which was once a self-guided tour but is now closed. In another 40 yards (37 m),

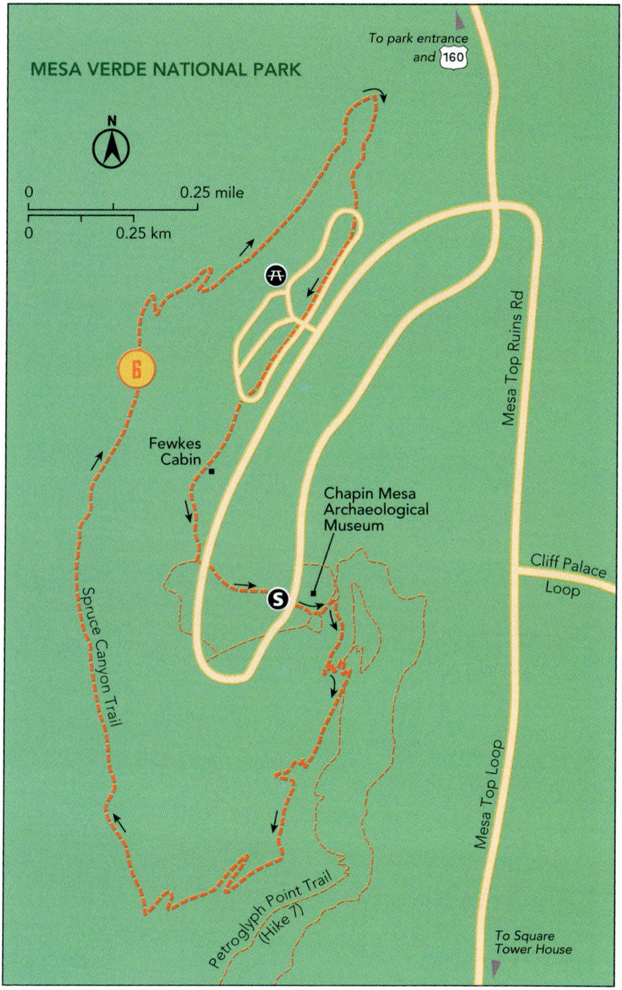

the pavement ends and the trail turns to dirt, switchbacking down farther into the canyon.

You reach the junction with the Petroglyph Point trail at 0.25 mile (0.4 km) or so to the left heading up. Continue

You can find solitude on the trail through Spruce Canyon.

straight on the Spruce Canyon Trail as it keeps descending. Navigate a big switchback at 0.3 mile (0.5 km) and cross a bridge shortly after. At just shy of 0.5 mile (0.8 km), there is a "nonpotable water" sign on the right, along with another bridge to cross.

Watch your head at 0.6 mile (0.9 km): you may have to duck under the rock outcropping on the left. Soon after, the trail opens up with views into Spruce Canyon. You may notice the solitude as you reach the canyon floor at 0.75 mile

(1.2 km). The woodlands habitat is a great place to observe wildlife, including Mesa Verde deer.

Depending on the time of year, the canyon floor is a wetland area. A barbed-wire fence encloses an area to keep out of. Remnants of the old trail before reconstruction can be seen before you come upon a wooden sign pointing right to return to the trailhead and museum; continue straight ahead. The shade on the canyon floor begins to thin out as the trail climbs. Just past 1 mile (1.6 km), the trail flattens out again.

Scramble between some rocks on the right at 1.1 miles (1.8 km). Oaks of the shrub-steppe ecosystem line the trailside. Back on the canyon floor, the path narrows and becomes more wooded again. Views of the canyon walls are almost swallowed by vegetation from spring to fall.

Shy of 1.5 miles (2.4 km), the path goes through a wash that most likely will be dry. Rocks in between the trail add some depth. Tall boulders hug the trail on both sides, giving it more of canyon feel before the path gets steeper and begins to switchback. Log steps help keep the ascent more manageable. A cool "cave" on the left a little before 1.6 miles (2.5 km) is a place to stop and explore. Climb up on the rocks and drink some water.

The trail ascends over some slickrock and log steps as it continues to climb. Catch your breath and take in the view behind you. Evidence of the 2002 Long Mesa Fire can be seen in scorched trees as you make your way to the mesa top. The sandstone around Spruce Canyon changed

Intriguing rock formations can be found along the trail.

colors due to the fire retardant used to fight the fire, turning it reddish pink. Do you notice some of this discoloration?

The mesa top appears at about 1.9 miles (3 km). Once on the mesa, you'll see a museum sign and a trail map on the left. In this area, there is a prime example of turtleback weathering that occurs when rock (in this case, Cliffhouse Sandstone) erodes away, causing cracks due to pressure.

Follow the access road through the picnic area. You pass Fewkes Cabin on the left at 2.2 miles (3.5 km). The oldest historical structure in the park, the cabin has had a few purposes, from ranger station to museum. Named after former superintendent of Mesa Verde National Park J. Walter Fewkes, it is no longer open to the public, as it serves as a ranger station again. Continue on the trail until you return to the museum. Remember to sign out of the registry.

7 PETROGLYPH POINT TRAIL

Distance: 2.4 miles (3.8 km)
Elevation gain: 174 feet (53 m)
High point: 6953 feet (2119 m)
Difficulty: Moderate
Trail surface: Dirt, slickrock, pavement
Map: Trails Illustrated Mesa Verde
GPS: 38.592236°N, 109.3838341°W
Note: Dogs prohibited; restrooms, water access in parking area and museum

The Petroglyph Point Trail is rugged, rocky, and often steep, requiring some scrambling. Pick up an interpretive pamphlet as you descend the paved trail to help identify interesting things along the way. Kids enjoy climbing rocks and searching for hidden sites. However, there is some climbing, tight spaces, and exposure, so hiking with a child in a backpack

The 35-foot-wide petroglyph panel features a mix of animal and human figures, handprints and spirals.

or carrier would be challenging. The trail is mostly shaded in the morning.

GETTING THERE

From the town of Cortez, head east on US 160 for almost 10 miles (16 km). Take the exit toward Mesa Verde National Park and turn right onto Mesa Top Ruins Road, the main park road. Follow the road south for 20 miles (32 km) to the all-way stop. Turn right and follow this one-way loop road for 0.7 mile (1.1 km) to the parking area and trailhead near Chapin Mesa Archaeological Museum.

ON THE TRAIL

There are two ways to hike this interpretive trail. One is to hike the loop clockwise, heading north from the Chapin Mesa Archaeological Museum and across the mesa top. This hike goes counterclockwise, starting down the paved path that takes you into Spruce Canyon (Hike 6). Either way, at the

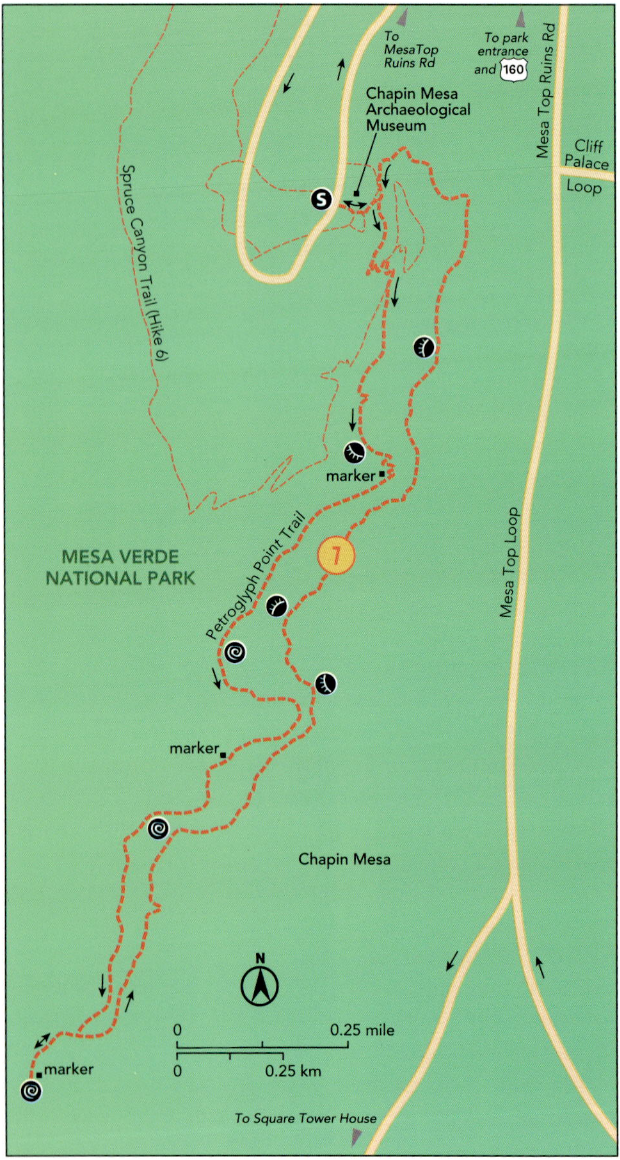
To MesaTop Ruins Rd
To park entrance and 160
Mesa Top Ruins Rd
Chapin Mesa Archaeological Museum
Cliff Palace Loop
Spruce Canyon Trail (Hike 6)
marker
Petroglyph Point Trail
7
MESA VERDE NATIONAL PARK
Mesa Top Loop
marker
Chapin Mesa
N
0
0.25 mile
0
0.25 km
marker
To Square Tower House

museum, sign the registry, then follow the signs for Spruce Tree House along the paved path.

At a little over 0.1 mile (0.2 km), you pass the side trail on the left to Spruce Tree House, which was once a self-guided tour but is now closed. In another 40 yards (37 m), the pavement ends and the trail turns to dirt, switchbacking down as you head farther into the canyon.

You come to a fork at 0.25 mile (0.4 km) with a sign that points up to the left for the Petroglyph Point Trail; take this, not the trail straight ahead, which is the Spruce Canyon Trail (Hike 6).

A little beyond 0.4 mile (0.7 km), there is a very short slot of rock to climb through, soon followed by open views of Spruce Canyon on the right. The trail turns to slickrock stairs after these views, then begins to head down. At 0.5 mile (0.8 km), markers No. 10 and 11 designate an old dwelling.

As you continue on the trail, you come to an overhang at 0.75 mile (1.2 km). In about 80 yards (73 m), an interesting rock feature may invite a stop for a quick drink as you take a look at it. You begin to see ant mite holes in the outcroppings and descend some stairs at 0.8 mile (1.3 km). What remains of some kivas are worth a stop for a look at a little past 0.9 mile (1.5 km), markers No. 17 and 18 in the pamphlet.

Be on the lookout for petroglyph sites on the left-hand side of the trail at around 1 mile (1.6 km). You have to climb up a bit to see them, but it is worth a stop. Rocks continue to tighten around you, and stairs climb up as you meander through scrub oak and pines.

At about 1.4 miles (2.2 km), a side trail of about 120 yards (110 m) leads to marker No. 24 at a 35-foot-wide (10 m) panel with more than thirty animal figures, handprints, and spirals. According to a Hopi elder, it may tell the story of the Mountain Sheep and Eagle Clans returning to their place of origin. Remember that this is a protected site. Do not touch the panel; just view it from afar.

Hidden sites can be found along the trail if you keep your eyes open.

Return to the main loop trail at a little over 1.5 miles (2.4 km); it now climbs 100 feet (30 m) with steep steps for perhaps the most difficult part of the hike as it leads you up to the Chapin Mesa top. Here the trail becomes a mix of dirt and gravel as it meanders across the mesa through spruce trees and other vegetation.

At around 1.7 miles (2.7 km), there is a nice viewpoint. Take some time to look at the vistas across the canyon. At 1.8 miles (2.9 km), you can see the museum as you stand basically right above Spruce Tree House.

Some slickrock descends at 2 miles (3.2 km). At this point, you can see some of the geological features in the park. Be on the lookout for concretions, masses of minerals that form around rock. They resemble elongated peach pits or coffee beans.

Shortly after, to the left are some glimpses of Spruce Tree House. In this area, there is a prime example of turtle-back weathering, made when rock (in this case Cliff House Sandstone) erodes away, causing cracks in the rock due to pressure. The trail continues along the slickrock and climbs back up toward the museum.

At about 2.3 miles (3.7 km), you reach the paved trail that leads back to the trailhead and parking area. Be sure to sign out at the museum registry when you finish your hike.

8 SQUARE TOWER HOUSE

Distance: 1 mile (1.6 km)
Elevation gain: 100 feet (30 m)
High point: 6857 feet (2090 m)
Difficulty: Moderate
Trail surface: Pavement, dirt, slickrock, ladders
Map: Trails Illustrated Mesa Verde
GPS: 38.5838512°N, 109.3838349°W
Note: Guided-tour reservation required; dogs prohibited; restrooms, water access at trailhead

> Square Tower House, the park's tallest structure, stands almost 30 feet (9.1 m) tall. There is only one ranger-guided tour per day, which must be booked in advance; it is a difficult ticket to get. Visitors must be able to navigate the uneven terrain and exposure without assistance, descending 100 feet (30 m), climbing ladders, and scrambling. There is little to no shade, so come prepared with water. The weather-dependent hike is available from mid-May to mid-October.

GETTING THERE

From the town of Cortez, head east on US 160 for almost 10 miles (16 km). Take the exit toward Mesa Verde National Park and turn right onto Mesa Top Ruins Road, the main park road. Follow the road south for 20.4 miles (33 km), through the all-way stop to the fork with the Cliff Palace Loop Road to the left. Continue straight on the Mesa Top

Square Tower is the tallest dwelling in the park.

Loop road for 1.5 miles (2.4 km). The trailhead is on the right.

ON THE TRAIL

The hike to Square Tower House begins as a paved trail that takes you to a viewpoint about 500 feet (152 m) down the path—0.2 mile (0.3 km) roundtrip to the overlook and back. Surrounding the trail to the overlook is rich vegetation, from

Mormon tea to serviceberries. You may see flags marking different plant species, placed here by the naturalists to help identify plant types, whether invasive or not. The Ancestral Puebloans relied on edible plants in their daily lives. Spend some time taking in the views of Square Tower House from above and Navajo Canyon. (In case you cannot book the tour, check out the quite impressive view from the overlook.)

After you pass the overlook, the now dirt trail begins its descent into the canyon to a rock cliff. At this point, the ranger may stop to give instructions for the most heart-racing part of this 1-mile (1.6 km) roundtrip hike.

The trail begins to narrow, with steep drop-offs and switch-backs. Across Navajo Canyon, you can see Echo House. The hike descends two 20-foot (6 m) ladders bolted into the Cliff House Sandstone. As you descend the ladder, notice the indentations in the rock. They were a part of the Civilian

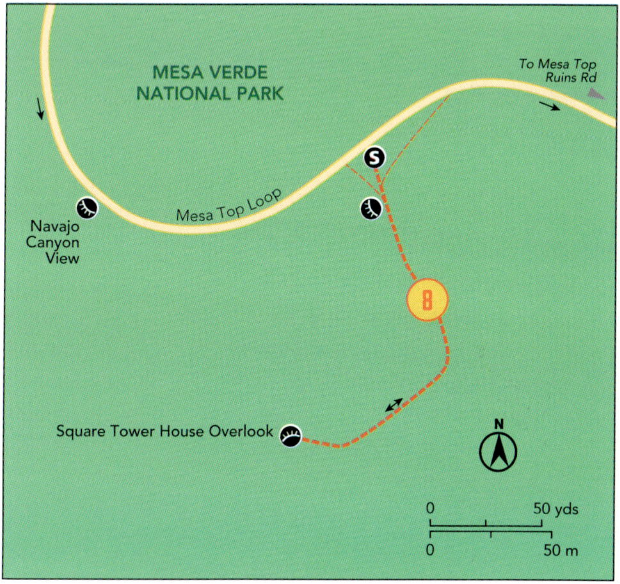

MESA TOP LOOP DRIVE AUDIO TOUR

Narrated by T.J. Atsye, a Mesa Verde National Park ranger and Laguna Pueblo Indian—a direct descendant of the people who used to live here—this forty-minute audio tour is the perfect companion to a drive on the 6-mile (10 km) Mesa Top Loop road. It explains the pit houses, pueblos, and sites on the mesa top. Learn more about Square Tower House, Oak Tree House, and more. You can search for the audio tour on the Mesa Verde National Park website or find the tour on Apple Podcasts.

Conservation Corps construction in the 1930s. When the backcountry tour program began at Mesa Verde in 2010, they installed the ladders for the safety of visitors who book a tour for an intimate view of Square Tower House. Wire fencing and ropes were installed to help with areas of exposure. The second ladder can make you feel like you are in a trust experiment. After descending stone steps, you must swing your leg over to meet the ladder. Ropes help you to keep your balance, but it still is a bit heart-racing.

After the ladders, a dirt trail takes you to the Square Tower House site. The tower is the tallest structure that has been found in the park, standing just shy of 30 feet (9 m). The ranger begins the tour working from left to right. One thing to notice is how shallow the alcove is where Square Tower House was built. It is much shallower than at other sites. To maximize space, the Puebloans built up. The ranger also points out the variations in plaster colors from white to buff. If not for the guide, you could miss the faint No. 8 (for Nordenskiöld No. 8) and the initials J W—John Wetherill.

To the right of the tower, a kiva has half its roof still intact. As of this writing, some stabilization and structural engineering was taking place at the site. While some sites do have

Hikers can see an overview of Square Tower from the viewpoint.

restoration projects with strict standards, today's Pueblo people feel that damage is part of the natural process. A boulder broke off years ago at Square Tower House, causing still-visible damage to some of the walls.

Higher above the tower, you can view the "Crow's Nest," which is not visible from the overlook. Much debate remains on the purpose of this structure. Some historians feel that it may have been built as a lookout—a possible sign of conflict between villages.

In all, there were eight kivas and between forty-nine and sixty rooms at the Square Tower House site. Wooden beams used for structural integrity are still sticking out of many walls. Shards of pottery, tools, and even corncobs can be found all around when exploring. It is okay to look at them, but they must remain at the site.

When the tour is over, you backtrack to the trailhead. The way back up is no easy task. The climb may take your breath away as you ascend out of the canyon. The tour returns to its start, concluding this ranger-guided hike that gives you an intimate view into the lives of the Ancestral Puebloans.

9 CLIFF PALACE OVERVIEW

Distance: 0.4 mile (0.6 km) plus house tour
Elevation gain: 115 feet (35 m)
High point: 6800 feet (2072 m)
Difficulty: Moderate
Trail surface: Pavement, dirt, ladder
Map: Trails Illustrated Mesa Verde
GPS: 38.584063°N, 109.3838349°W
Note: Guided-tour reservation required; dogs prohibited; restroom, water access at trailhead

> Cliff Palace, the largest cliff dwelling in North America, is famous around the world and has become a symbol of Ancestral Puebloan architecture. Built between CE 1190 and 1280, it is believed to have been home to a hundred people and contained 150 rooms and 23 kivas. Because of its size, archaeologists believe that Cliff Palace may have been a religious, cultural, or administrative center. Reservations for a ranger-assisted tour are required for this hike.

Cliff Palace is the largest dwelling in the park.

A view of Cliff Palace from the overlook shows the impressive size of the site.

GETTING THERE

From the town of Cortez, head east on US 160 for almost 10 miles (16 km). Take the exit toward Mesa Verde National Park and turn right onto Mesa Top Ruins Road, the main park road. Follow the road south for 20.4 miles (33 km), through the all-way stop to the fork with the Mesa Top Loop road to the right. Turn left onto Cliff Palace Loop road (Mesa Top Ruins Road) and follow it 1.7 miles (2.7 km) to the parking lot.

ON THE TRAIL

This ranger-assisted tour begins with a walk along a paved path for a short distance to the Cliff Palace overlook. Stop by the shack for a pamphlet and a bottle of water as you make your way to the overlook. Note that the shack may not be staffed at all times. From the overlook, a ranger meets you to discuss the hike, safety guidelines, and rules. The guide then leads you down a staircase through a narrow opening between the Cliff House Sandstone to a locked gate, then

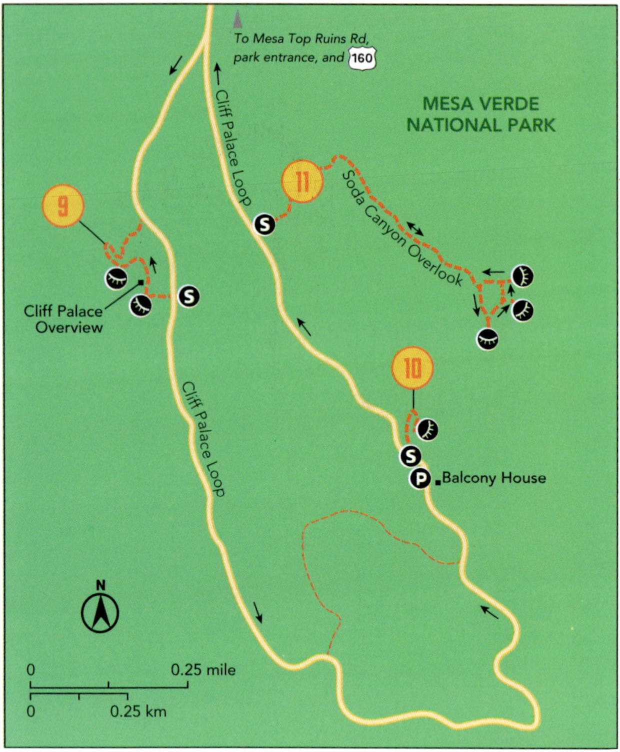

takes you into and out of the site. Bring a list of questions, as the ranger taking you through the dwelling shares their vast knowledge.

From the gate, you descend 150 feet (46 m) to the site. Steel steps and a short 8- to 10-foot (2–3 m) ladder bring you down to the up-close viewing area of Cliff Palace. Depending on how quickly your group gets down into the site, you typically have thirty minutes or so to take in the dwelling. Expect to come upon other tours as you move to various points in the viewing area. The ranger talks in detail about Cliff Palace, its creation, and the stabilization efforts to preserve the site.

As you move through the tour, look down into the kivas for a view into the ceremonial life of the Ancestral Puebloans. Notice the different colors of plaster used to create the walls. Can you imagine squeezing through the holes to get from room to room or climbing ladders and walls to get to the rooms above? You will leave this tour impressed with the resourcefulness of the Puebloans.

The trail back up and out of the canyon is the hardest part of this hike. It requires you to climb uneven stone steps and three ladders, as well as squeeze through some tight rock enclosures. The tour ends when you return to the parking lot.

10 BALCONY HOUSE

Distance: 0.4 mile (0.6 km) plus house tour
Elevation gain: 150 feet (45 m)
High point: 6800 feet (2072 m)
Difficulty: Moderate
Trail surface: Dirt, slickrock, ladder
Map: Trails Illustrated Mesa Verde
GPS: 38.5788144°N, 109.3838354°W
Note: Guided-tour reservation required; dogs prohibited; restrooms, water access at trailhead

Balcony House, a medium-size dwelling, contains forty rooms, kivas (two well-preserved), and plazas. The one-hour, ranger-guided tour, offered mid-May through October, is the most challenging and exposed in the park. Visitors climb multiple ladders, descend steps, and climb and crawl through a 12-foot by 18-inch (3.7-m by 46-cm) tunnel. You will need to keep your hands free throughout the tour. Food and drinks, except water, are prohibited, to keep rodents from entering and damaging the site. (See map in Hike 9.)

This viewpoint shows you how big some of the kivas were.

GETTING THERE

From the town of Cortez, head east on US 160 for almost 10 miles (16 km). Take the exit toward Mesa Verde National Park and turn right onto Mesa Top Ruins Road, the main park road. Follow the road south for 20.4 miles (33 km), through the all-way stop to the fork with the Mesa Top Loop road to the right. Stay left on Cliff Palace Loop road (Mesa Top Ruins Road) and follow it for 3.4 miles (5.5 km) to the parking lot.

ON THE TRAIL

In the spring of 1884, prospector S. E. Osborn was the first European to enter Balcony House, while archaeologist Jesse Nusbaum excavated the area in 1910. You can see the village site from a distance on the Soda Canyon Overlook trail (Hike 11), but the only true way to see the site is by booking a ranger-guided tour. From the parking area, the route to Balcony House begins descending into Soda Canyon. The first obstacle you encounter is a set of stairs that brings you to below the parking area.

After the stairs, a fairly wide concrete path descends gradually and flattens out. A small seep stream can be seen on the right-hand side, most likely a source of water for the Ancestral Puebloans. After the seep, the trail leads to a set of stairs that take you to the first of several ladders of different lengths. Depending on tour size, the 32-foot-long (9.8 m) ladder usually is accessed two at a time. Bolted tightly, the ladder doesn't move as visitors climb it. You will get your first peek at the site as you ascend the ladder.

A narrow, dark passage leads to the balcony of Balcony House. The balcony sets this site apart from others within the park: it provides views of Soda Canyon. Many passageways were bricked off to make them tighter and more tunnel-like as a form of defense. This tour allows visitors to walk through the rooms and plazas with discretion.

This is one of the ladders on the Balcony House tour.

As you climb through the tight passageways, marvel at the craftsmanship and attention to detail the Ancestral Puebloans put into the site. Brick and mortar, wood beams, and the already-in-place alcoves were all essential tools in the building of the dwellings. Small ladders take you in and out of the relatively well-preserved rooms and to the back rooms that were most likely used in colder weather. The blackened walls are evidence of fires that were probably built to keep the Puebloans warm and to cook in winter. Archaeologists believe two families may have lived here.

Kivas now wide open once featured tops to them. You may find pottery and other artifacts along the trail and at the pit-house sites. The artifacts are protected by law and must remain at the site.

Visitors exit the site by a combination of steps and ladders. Fencing and chains are an extra safety feature. One last ladder brings the guided hike back to the parking lot.

Ladders take you into different levels of rooms.

11 SODA CANYON OVERLOOK

Distance: 1.2 miles (1.9 km)
Elevation gain: 173 feet (52 m)
High point: 6850 feet (2090 m)
Difficulty: Easy
Trail surface: Dirt, slickrock, stairs
Map: Trails Illustrated Mesa Verde
GPS: 37.167557°N, 108.4724474°W
Note: Dogs prohibited; restrooms, water access at Balcony House tour parking area

> This fairly level trail, the only one with a view of Balcony House without a tour, visits three overlooks of Balcony House and Soda Canyon. Bring binoculars for a better look. Good for a variety of ages and mobility levels, it is open 8 AM to sunset, late spring to the first significant snowfall. The best times are mornings or evenings, May through October. When groomed in winter, it is open to cross-country skiers and snowshoers. (See map in Hike 9.)

GETTING THERE

From the town of Cortez, head east on US 160 for almost 10 miles (16 km). Take the exit toward Mesa Verde National Park and turn right onto Mesa Top Ruins Road, the main park road. Follow the road south for 20.4 miles (33 km), through the all-way stop to the fork with the Mesa Top Loop road to the right. Stay left on Cliff Palace Loop road (Mesa Top Ruins Road) and follow it for 3.9 miles (6.3 km) to the trailhead just past the parking area for Balcony House (Hike 10). Be prepared to park on the side of the road.

ON THE TRAIL

This out-and-back hike begins on a wide trail through piñon and junipers. At a little over 0.1 mile (0.2 km), navigate the rock stairs as you descend toward the overlooks. From the start, the trail is easy to follow, rolling along beside cactus and shrubs including Mormon tea. You may find some shady relief on this hike, but for the most part it is in the sun.

At 0.5 mile (0.8 km), an arrow on a wood post directs you to the right to begin the loop toward the first overlook. At this junction, you can go clockwise or counterclockwise. There is no significant advantage to either direction, but you may be able to escape the crowds by tackling the trail clockwise. Keeping with the typical traffic flow, this hike heads to the right to hike the loop counterclockwise.

The trail opens up more as you come upon the overlook for Balcony House in about 100 yards (91 m) from the signpost.

Balcony House can be seen in detail through a viewfinder at the overlook.

WILDFIRES

Due to the presence of archaeological sites, Mesa Verde has not implemented a controlled-burn program like other national parks. Therefore, two-thirds of the park has burned in wildfires over the past couple of decades, with some fires coming dangerously close to structures. About 95 percent of the fires in the park boundary have been caused by lightning burning juniper, mountain shrub, and piñon. The park has averaged nineteen lightning wildfires a year since the last big fire in 2003.

From this overlook, gaze to the right into the canyon to see a faraway view of Balcony House. After taking in the vista (did you remember to bring binoculars?), follow the loop to the left to continue to the Soda Canyon overlook. In another 90 yards (82 m) or so, a wooden sign directs you down some rock steps to the second overlook, which takes you about 30 feet (9.1 m) out into the canyon.

A viewfinder allows you to get a closer look at the dwelling if you didn't bring any binoculars. Can you see anyone enjoying a booked tour of Balcony House? The ladders are a good place to spot someone. From this unique perspective, imagine life as a Puebloan from this dwelling. Can you see the telltale balcony that gave this site its name?

Keep an eye out for birds of prey soaring above the canyon walls. Turkey vultures, kestrels, and ravens can often be seen flying over the canyon looking for a meal. Jackrabbits may bolt across the trail, along with lizards and even the occasional prairie snakes. Deer and mountain lions call the mesa area home too.

Do you notice the white calcium-carbonate deposits that gave the canyon its name? You can also look across the

The Soda Canyon Trail offers a full view of the canyon.

canyon with the scope and your binoculars to see another unnamed site below an area of scorched trees from the Bircher Fire in 2000.

After leaving the second viewpoint, follow the loop about 100 yards (91 m) until you reach the third overlook. This viewpoint with a different look into the canyon might provide a better place to see the calcium deposits.

After drinking in the views of Soda Canyon, continue to follow the loop counterclockwise. At 0.7 mile (1.1 km), the loop meets back up with the main trail. Retrace your steps to the trailhead.

WETHERILL MESA

The Wetherill Mesa region forms the lowest forest zone in the Rocky Mountains, with Rock Canyon the most wide open of the mesa tops. The Pony Fire in 2000 burned much of the landscape, evident by the many charred piñon pines and juniper trees that remain. The area is slowly regrowing, but don't be surprised by the lack of vegetation. Still, the red soil called loess proved to be wonderful for farming during Ancestral Puebloan times, so new growth will continue in the area.

The Wetherill Mesa Road begins in the Far View area, heading west, then south to the road's end in 12 miles (19 km). Along the way are overlooks: Window to the Past, Fire Recovery Viewpoint, McElmo Canyon View, and Rock Canyon Tower View. At the road's end you'll find a ranger station, cafe, picnic area, and restrooms. The Wetherill Mesa area, the quietest, least-visited area of Mesa Verde National Park, is open only from mid- to end of April through October, weather dependent, while some hikes are open mid-May through October. Also, the Wetherill Mesa area is open only until sunset, so keep that in mind when making park plans.

RESTORED REMAINS AND ARTIFACTS

While numerous protections have kept visitors from stealing artifacts since Mesa Verde was named a national park, geologist and Swedish nobleman Gustaf Nordenskiöld

OPPOSITE: *The trail changes to paved as you get closer to Step House.*

(pronounced Nordensholt or Nürdenhoeld) did take artifacts from the area during his work with a crew to document the visible dwelling at Nordenskiöld No. 16 in 1891, with the guidance of the Wetherill family. Human remains and objects commemorating the deceased were sold to a Finnish doctor. These artifacts were in the National Museum of Finland in Helsinki for 129 years. In autumn 2020 when the human remains were returned, descendants of the Ancestral Puebloans performed a ceremony to rebury twenty humans and the funerary items.

12 STEP HOUSE LOOP

Distance: 1 mile (1.6 km) plus exploring
Elevation gain: 100 feet (52 m)
High point: 7300 feet (2225 m)
Difficulty: Moderate
Trail surface: Dirt, gravel, concrete, slickrock, stairs
Map: Trails Illustrated Mesa Verde
GPS: 37.167557°N, 108.4724474°W
Note: Dogs prohibited; restrooms, water access near parking lot

> Step House, one of the park's few self-guided tours, is also one of its most unusual sites, because it shows two separate occupations. This interpretive hike with a 100-foot (30 m) descent and ascent is more moderate because of the elevation and desert heat. Signs explain the lush vegetation that escaped wildfire damage. Grab a brochure to identify the pueblos and prehistoric steps. Ask rangers questions while you respectfully visit the dwellings. (See map in Hike 13.)

GETTING THERE

From the town of Cortez, head east on US 160 for almost 10 miles (16 km). Take the exit toward Mesa Verde National

The Step House Village saw two different occupations: Basketmaker III and Pueblo III.

Park and turn right onto Mesa Top Ruins Road, the main park road. Follow the road south for almost 15 miles (24 km) to the Wetherill Mesa sign (near mile marker 15) and turn right. Follow the Wetherill Mesa Road for 12 miles (19 km) to the parking area at the road's end.

ON THE TRAIL

Step House is open only seasonally, from mid-May to mid-September, when staffed by a ranger. The gate is typically open from 9 or 10 AM to 3:30 or 4 PM. If the gate area is closed, there is no staffing and Step House is closed. Check for times when making your park visitation plans.

The trail to the self-guided tour of Step House begins from the parking lot and information area. Cross the paved road (now a walking path) and locate the wooden sign on the left for Step House. The trail begins as gravel and dirt and crosses the mesa top, where evidence of the 2000 Pony

A pueblo at Step House

Fire can be seen. At 0.1 mile (0.2 km) from the trailhead, you come to a fork. From here you can go clockwise or counterclockwise. This hike goes counterclockwise to begin with the descent, which provides a more dramatic view of the site as you head down into the canyon, so at the fork, go straight.

The first informational sign points out the Utah juniper. The trail turns from gravel to paved. Stairs bring you down from the rim and deeper into Long Canyon. A few more informational signs appear, typically on the left, including text about snowberries. The first peekaboo views of Step House are to the right through the dense vegetation, including Oregon grape and skunkbush.

At 0.4 mile (0.6 km), you come upon Step House. The area is free to explore with posted restrictions. One of the best-preserved negative handprints (images of hands made by putting pigment on a hand and pressing it against a rock surface) can be found at Step House. Can you spot the negative handprint? If not, a ranger can surely help you.

In early CE 600s, a Basketmaker III pit-house community occupied the area, while in the 1200s, a Pueblo III community did so. There are six known Basketmaker III pit structures and a Pueblo III masonry pueblo with twenty-seven rooms and three kivas. It is thought that the pueblos were not discovered during the first excavation, by Gustaf Nordenskiöld, but rather were first discovered in 1926 by Park Superintendent Jesse L. Nusbaum and his crew that excavated the first three pit houses. It wasn't until 1962 when working on a stabilization project that Robert Nichols and Al Lancaster found the last of the pueblos.

Can you tell the difference in the craftsmanship and materials used between the two occupation periods? If you have questions or couldn't grab a brochure, the rangers onsite are great at answering questions.

Climb the ladder to the path that takes you to the upper area of Step House. See the kivas up close. Use the informational brochure to help identify the numbered signage. Sign No. 1 designates what is left of a stone stairway used to access the different levels in the alcove. This discovery was how Step House got its name.

LOOK FOR COLOR

While the stonework of the ancient dwellings is impressive, don't miss observing the color on some of the stones throughout Mesa Verde National Park and Canyons of the Ancients and Hovenweep National Monuments. The colors, including blue, yellow, and black, are actually plaster colored with pigments made from what was found around the Puebloans: charcoal, flowers, and more. Much like paint is used to decorate today, plaster was used in Ancestral Puebloan time as art and also to help protect the walls from the elements.

Some other favorite tidbits are found at signs No. 3 and 4. At No. 3, you can see where Nordenskiöld inscribed "No. 21" into the rock, his site number for this area. In the same rock face, you can see where the Ancestral Puebloans used the rock to shape and sharpen the stone tools they used.

No. 4 requires you to climb a short ladder. At its top, you can see a set of petroglyphs. Modern Pueblo people describe the symbols as migration and clan symbols: human figures, geometric designs, and animals.

Peer inside the pueblos and look at the care that has been taken to stabilize the dwellings for future generations to experience as well. The kivas were fully plastered. A painted panel of bighorn sheep was found at the kiva at sign No. 6. The panel was removed in 1989 and placed in curation for protection.

After spending some time exploring Step House, return to the trail and drink some water before you begin climbing back up the canyon on the shade-free ascent of the paved path and stairs. Be aware that people may be coming down as you go up. Depending on how much exploring you do, you encounter the fork once again at around 0.8 mile (1.4 km). Head to the right to return to the trailhead.

13 NORDENSKIÖLD SITE NO. 16 TRAIL

Distance: 2 miles (3.2 km)
Elevation gain: 95 feet (29 m)
High point: 7300 feet (2225 m)
Difficulty: Easy
Trail surface: Gravel, slickrock, stairs
Map: Trails Illustrated Mesa Verde
GPS: 37.2013833°N, 108.5523346°W
Note: Leashed dogs allowed; restrooms, water access at trailhead

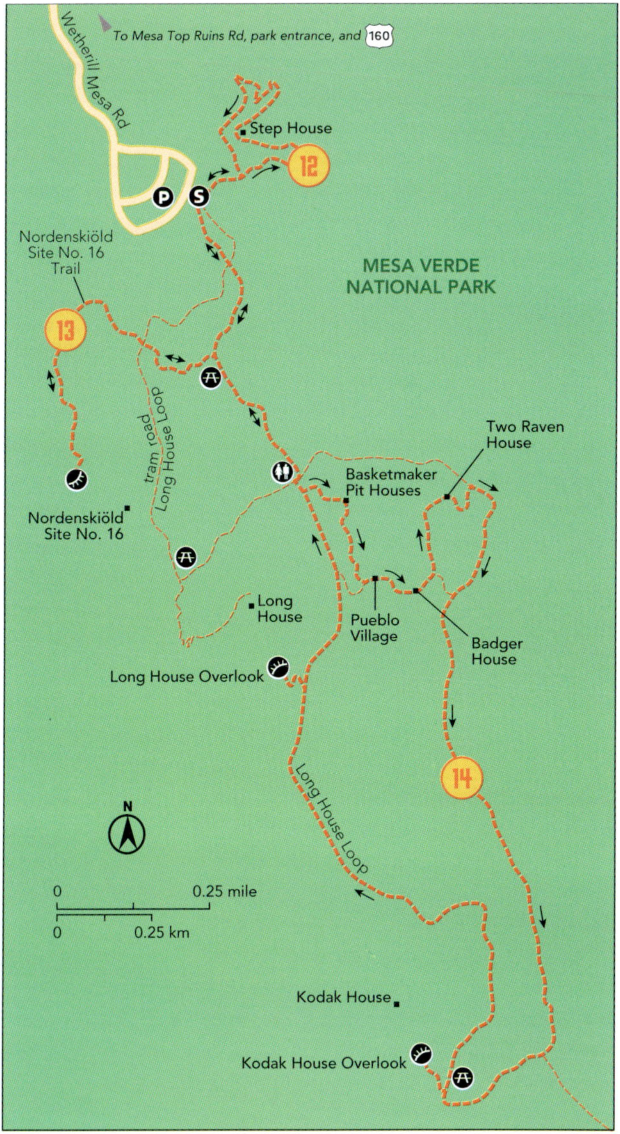
To Mesa Top Ruins Rd, park entrance, and 160
Wetherill Mesa Rd
Step House
12
P
S
Nordenskiöld Site No. 16 Trail
13
MESA VERDE NATIONAL PARK
tram road
Long House Loop
Two Raven House
Basketmaker Pit Houses
Nordenskiöld Site No. 16
Long House
Pueblo Village
Badger House
Long House Overlook
14
Long House Loop
N
0
0.25 mile
0
0.25 km
Kodak House
Kodak House Overlook

Nordenskiöld Site No. 16 is named after geologist Gustaf Nordenskiöld, who in 1891 worked with a crew, with the guidance of the Wetherill family, to document the visible dwelling. Seen from a viewpoint across Rock Canyon, the dwelling contains a tower, several kivas, communal areas, and thirty-nine rooms. It is a prime example of blending a dwelling with its surroundings for defensive purposes. Bring water on this hike, as there is no shade.

GETTING THERE

From the town of Cortez, head east on US 160 for almost 10 miles (16 km). Take the exit toward Mesa Verde National Park and turn right onto Mesa Top Ruins Road, the main park road. Follow the road south for almost 15 miles (24 km) to the Wetherill Mesa sign (near mile marker 15) and turn right. Follow the Wetherill Mesa Road for 12 miles (19 km) to the parking area at the road's end.

ON THE TRAIL

From the Wetherill Mesa kiosk and ranger station, follow the gravel trail south. At about 0.1 mile (0.2 km), the trail crosses the tram road. As of this writing, the tram is not running, but it is always good practice to look both ways when crossing a road.

Follow the trail until, at 0.3 mile (0.5 km), the gravel trail splits at a sign for the Nordenskiöld Site No. 16 Trail. The left fork heads to Badger House and part of the Long House Loop (Hike 14); turn right for this hike to the Nordenskiöld Site No. 16 overlook.

You may be surprised by wild horses that might be seen along the trail. They could be your only companions here. The expanse of land provides good views of many desert creatures. Snakes, including bull snakes and rattlers, love the hot desert habitat, as do a variety of lizards.

Nordenskiöld Site No. 16 can be seen from the trail overlook.

Be sure you take in water on this short hike. There is absolutely no shade, though new growth of piñon pines and other vegetation continues to thrive once again in the area burned by the 2000 Pony Fire. Continue to follow the trail a short 0.2 mile (0.3 km) to where it once again crosses the road at a tram stop at a little shy of 0.6 mile (0.9 km) from the trailhead.

As you continue to cross the mesa top of Rock Canyon for a short 0.5 mile (0.8 km), be on the lookout for the site. At approximately 1 mile (1.6 km) from the trailhead, steps take

A LIVING PART OF CULTURE

Modern Indian tribes find a deep connection to the spirits that once inhabited the sites found in Mesa Verde National Park and Canyons of the Ancients and Hovenweep National Monuments. Stories told by tradition explain a life full of trials, tribulations, and strength of family. What remains of these homes, including structures, seeps, and vegetation, are still regarded with great respect. The tribes often visit these sites to bless them to "keep these places warm," as the National Conservation Lands brochure for Sand Canyon states.

you down to an overlook area of slickrock and dirt. Hopefully you packed your binoculars, as this site can be seen only across Rock Canyon. While you look across the canyon at the dwelling, picture yourself living with two or three families there.

With an estimated twenty to thirty people living here at one time, the privacy and space can today be compared to individuals living in a tiny house. It puts life back then into perspective. What do you think communal rooms were used for back then? Would we use communal rooms for the same things today? Notice the two-level structure—it takes advantage of the taller alcove. Notice how the dwelling blends in with the scenery, no doubt a defensive mechanism.

From Nordenskiöld's findings, it was concluded that the modern Hopi and the ancient Mesa Verde inhabitants are closely related. Looking to the right, you can also see the Ute Mountain Tribal Park across the canyon.

Head back the way you came to retrace your steps, following the signs to return to the Wetherill Mesa information center and parking lot.

14 LONG HOUSE LOOP

Distance: 4.3 miles (6.9 km)
Elevation gain: 285 feet (86 m)
High point: 7218 feet (2200 m)
Difficulty: Easy
Trail surface: Gravel, pavement
Map: Trails Illustrated Mesa Verde
GPS: 37.2013833°N, 108.5523346°W
Note: Leashed dogs allowed; restrooms, water access at trailhead

> This loop across Wetherill Mesa follows the defunct tram route, which bicyclists still use. This self-guided hike visits Badger House, plus Kodak House and Long House Overlooks. Educational signage explains life for the Ancestral Puebloans. The tours of Long House often fill up fast, but this alternative trail allows you to view the dwelling from a distance. The loop is open May through October, weather dependent. There is no shade, so bring water and a hat. (See map in Hike 13.)

GETTING THERE

From the town of Cortez, head east on US 160 for almost 10 miles (16 km). Take the exit toward Mesa Verde National Park and turn right onto Mesa Top Ruins Road, the main park road. Follow the road for almost 15 miles (24 km) to the Wetherill Mesa sign (near mile marker 15) and turn right. Follow the Wetherill Mesa Road for 12 miles (19 km) to the parking area at the road's end.

ON THE TRAIL

From the Wetherill Mesa kiosk and ranger station, follow the gravel trail past the sign for Step House (Hike 12) and continue south toward Badger House. At about 0.1 mile (0.2

km), the trail crosses the tram road. Continue on the dirt trail toward Badger House.

At 0.25 mile (0.4 km), reach a junction. The trail to the right leads to the Nordenskiöld Site No. 16 Trail (Hike 13); look for a sign to Badger House and head left. This flat section of trail, about 0.25 mile (0.4 km), often sees two-way traffic between people and dogs as it passes a picnic area, restrooms, and a tram stop or two.

At 0.6 mile (0.8 km), shortly after the trail crosses the tram road again, it reaches a junction; head left for the Badger House Community, which consists of four excavated sites under rooftop protection: Modified Basketmaker Pit Houses, Developmental Pueblo Village, Badger House, and Two Raven House. Shortly after crossing the tram road, the first of the four sites appears. The Modified Basketmaker Pit Houses (CE 650) were home to many Ancestral Puebloans and contained aboveground storage rooms made from mud plaster. This area is a walk through time as human life developed in the Mesa Verde area.

From the pit houses, continue south on the path for another 0.2 mile (0.3 km) to the pueblo village (a short side trail to the right connects to the Long House Loop tram road). The Developmental Pueblo Village (CE 750) shows some of the earliest masonry work for the Puebloans. It is estimated that the site was occupied for more than three hundred years and contained one great kiva.

From the pueblo village, head left on the path about 0.1 mile (0.2 km) to Badger House, said to have been occupied from approximately CE 900 to 1200. Outside of Badger House is a tower possibly used for safety and communication, connected by a 41-foot-long (12.5 m) underground tunnel to the rooms. Two kivas and many rooms are still standing today. The house was given its name because when it was excavated, a large number of badger holes were found in trash piles at the site. It is believed that many materials, including

Two Raven House was found by Dr. Jerry Melbye in May 1960 during an archaeological survey.

wood beams and stones, were removed by the Puebloans to help them build Long House and Kodak House.

From Badger House, continue on the trail a short way to a junction with another short side trail to the Long House Loop tram road; continue straight for the last stop in the Badger Community, a little over 0.2 mile (0.3 km) from Badger House: Two Raven House. It was found in the sagebrush in May 1960 during an archaeological survey by Dr. Jerry Melbye, founder of University of Toronto Mississauga's forensic science program, during his work on the Wetherill Mesa Project.

Occupied from CE 900 to 1100, Two Raven House is one of the few sites in the American Southwest to feature a palisade—a fence made from posts and brush. This may have been used to keep domesticated turkeys in place and also as a windbreak. Do you see how areas of the pit are reddened by fire? Archaeologists believe that is because it was used as an oven. Short-wall rooms and a small kiva can be seen.

After visiting Two Raven House, follow the trail to the right. In less than 0.1 mile (0.2 km), you reach the Long House Loop tram road and a sign for the Long House and Kodak House Overlooks. If you need some quick shade, park yourself at the tram stop, 1.2 miles (1.9 km) from the trailhead, to take in some water. Wild horses, chipmunks, and coyotes are commonly seen along the trail. To continue to the next stops, turn right (south) on the Long House Loop tram road.

Brown mile markers continue along the route. Areas of fire devastation can be seen on the right. In 0.2 mile (0.3 km) from the last tram stop is the short side trail back toward Badger House; as you continue south on the loop road, you can start to see cliff walls if you look far to the right.

At 2 miles (3.2 km), the smell of pine may greet you as the forest continues to grow and restore itself after the 2000 Pony Fire. Wildflowers including flowering cactus mix in with the pines.

At 2.2 miles (3.5 km), the trail bends to the southwest at another tram stop. In 0.2 mile (0.3 km), you come upon the overlook for Kodak House. Follow the path for about 90 yards (82 m) to the overlook. This is the only trail to view

The view into another part of Two Raven House

An overlook for Kodak House is along the loop.

Kodak House, a two-story dwelling that contains a large tower, kivas, and rooms. It was given its name because Gustaf Nordenskiöld would often leave his camera lying around as he moved between excavations in the area. Can you spot the tower? How do you think the Ancestral Puebloans were able to access this alcove?

Follow the overlook path back to the paved loop (you've now walked 2.5 miles (4 km) from the trailhead) and head to the left (north) to continue on to the Long House Overlook. At 3.4 miles (5.4 km), you can see a peekaboo view of Long House through the pines. About 0.1 mile (0.2 km) after the view, the overlook for Long House is on the left at 3.5 miles (5.6 km). Take the short winding path to the right 0.1 mile (0.2 km) to the overlook.

Long House was said to be a gathering place for trade. It is almost equal in size to Cliff Palace on Chapin Mesa. Containing 21 kivas, 150 rooms, and storage rooms, it is estimated to have been home to up to 175 people. Can you see people on a tour visiting the dwelling? Are you able to tell where the storage rooms are? Close your eyes. Do you see trades for goods occurring among families and possibly nomadic tribes?

Back on the road heading north, at around 3.6 miles (5.8 km), you come upon a short side trail on the right that leads to Badger House. Continue straight ahead on the trail back to the tram stop at the crossing of the tram road at 3.9 miles (6.3 km). Cross the road onto the trail and leave the pavement behind. On the left at a little over 4 miles (6.4 km), you pass the trail for the Nordenskiöld Site No. 16 Trail (Hike 13). Continue to the right on the gravel path to the trailhead at about 4.3 miles (6.9 km).

OPPOSITE: *The Big Al Trail is surrounded by aspens and Gambel oak.*

PART 2: MANCOS, CORTEZ, AND DOLORES

OVERVIEW OF MANCOS, CORTEZ, AND DOLORES
SAN JUAN NATIONAL FOREST
Dunton
23
Geyser Creek
Forest Road 535
West Dolores River
To Telluride
145
Dolores River
Dolores River
McPhee Reservoir
To Monticello, UT
145
491
Lewis
22
Dolores
21
184
561
Transfer Campground
16
17
350
W Mancos R
Jackson Creek Reservoir
42
18
Weber Reservoir
15
44
Middde Mancos River
184
491
145
29
20
Cortez
19
160
Oak St
Mancos
160
G
To Aneth, UT
To Durango
MESA VERDE NATIONAL PARK
160
491
N
To Shiprock, AZ
0
10 miles
0
10 kms
Mancos River
COLORADO
NEW MEXICO

MANCOS

The town of Mancos, on US 160 at State Highway 184, has a long history—from Ancestral Puebloans to Native Americans, Spanish explorers to ranchers and miners. The Mancos River flows through the town and down into Mesa Verde National Park, which is about 7 miles (11 km) west of Mancos. Today the town has a lot of dining and lodging options, as well as outdoor activities ranging from hiking, bicycling, and skiing to fishing and horseback riding in areas including Mancos State Park, Rampart Hills, and the San Juan Mountains. The Mancos Valley Visitor Center is open April through October (see Appendix A: Resources for details), and two information kiosks provide year-round information.

15 MANCOS STATE PARK LOOP

Distance: 4.7 miles (7.5 km)
Elevation gain: 400 feet (121 m)
High point: 8245 feet (2513 m)
Difficulty: Easy
Trail surface: Dirt
Map: Trails Illustrated Durango Cortez
GPS: 38.6026965°N, 109.2751461°W
Note: Day-use fee or state parks pass required; leashed dogs allowed; restrooms at trailhead

The trail hugs Jackson Gulch Reservoir at the beginning and end of the hike.

A forested alternative to the desert hikes in the area, this lollipop hike (out to a loop and back) follows the Mule Deer, Mountain Lion, and Black Bear Trails in Mancos State Park. The trail hugs Jackson Gulch Reservoir before entering the forest. Bird-watchers will love looking for more than two hundred species of birds, including songbirds, raptors, and waterfowl. These multiuse trails shared with bikers and horses are open for snowshoeing and cross-country skiing in winter.

GETTING THERE

In Mancos, head north on N. Main Street (State Highway 184) from Grand Avenue (US 160 business loop). Continue north for 0.5 mile (0.8) km) and turn right onto County Road 42. At 3 miles (4.8 km), turn left to stay onto CR 42. In 1 mile (1.6 km) more, turn left onto CR N. Follow CR N about 0.5 mile (0.8 km) into the park and turn right to park at the first picnic area, near the Mule Deer trailhead.

ON THE TRAIL

From the Mule Deer trailhead, follow the Mule Deer Trail north as it winds above the shores of Jackson Gulch

Reservoir, known as Jackson Lake to locals. The trail is mostly doubletrack dirt and rock, but it may be overgrown in areas. Enjoy the views of the water and wildflowers lining the sides of the trail in the summer, including mountain mulberry, yarrow, and lupine. Oaks turn vibrant in the fall. Views of the La Plata Range of the San Juan Mountains are abundant as you make your way along the trail.

Don't be alarmed if you hear a chicken or other farm animal: the trail borders some farms on the right-hand side in

Watch for wildlife along the reservoir and in the forest too.

the beginning of this hike. Above the shoreline, the trail descends a bit as you continue north. This area can be wet and muddy especially after heavy rains or in the shoulder season. Many species of frogs and lizards can be found in the park. The area is also home to a wide variety of snakes, gophers, and small rodents. Bats are common in the evenings, as well as owls.

At 0.7 mile (1.1 km), you cross a small footbridge. Here a sign states that foot and bike traffic should use the bridge but horse traffic should go around it. The trail begins to head west. You reach the Quarry trailhead at 1 mile (1.6 km). Follow the Mountain Lion Trail, designated with a mountain lion paw sign, as it heads west. The trail travels past a picnic area and campsites as it hugs the west shoreline. You begin a short climb, and the path leads farther away from the shoreline through a forest. The ponderosa pines and other flora make this a perfect home for mule deer, elk, bobcats, bears, and moose.

After the easy climb, the trail levels off and reaches a junction with the Black Bear Trail at 1.5 miles (2.4 km). At the junction, you can head right or left to complete the loop of the Black Bear Trail; for this hike, take the Black Bear Trail to the right.

As you head north, then west on the trail, you may be able to spot Mesa Verde National Park in the distance. The Black Bear Trail is a moderate hike featuring more elevation change and loose terrain, including rocks. Expect to see downed trees and limbs (think hiking sticks) along this natural dirt trail. At a bit over 2.3 miles (3.7 km), at a junction with a trail heading right (north) into San Juan National Forest, stay left on the Black Bear Trail.

At around 2.7 miles (4.3 km) or so, reach another junction; the trail to the right leads south to the Chicken Creek trailhead, so stay left on the Black Bear Trail. At about 3.2 miles (5.1 km) you complete the Black Bear Trail loop and return to the junction with the Mountain Lion Trail.

Turn right onto the Mountain Lion Trail, headed east for the return. Retrace your steps to the Quarry trailhead at 3.7 miles (5.9 km) and head back on the Mule Deer Trail, crossing the footbridge, to reach the trailhead at 4.7 miles (7.5 km).

16 BIG AL TRAIL

Distance: 1.2 miles (1.9 km)
Elevation gain: 77 feet (23.5 m)
High point: 8980 feet (2737 m)
Difficulty: Easy
Trail surface: Gravel, dirt
Map: Trails Illustrated Durango Cortez
GPS: 37.4684581°N, 108.2103746°W
Note: Leashed dogs allowed; no water access

> This interpretive trail is ADA accessible, taking you through aspen groves with benches every 500 feet (152 m). Named for Al Lorentzen, who was injured fighting a fire near Yellowstone

In fall, aspens add glorious color along the Big Al Trail.

National Park in 1988, the trail to an overlook of the West Mancos River valley and Mount Hesperus has been adopted by the Adaptive Sports Association in Durango. While you can hike this trail in less than forty-five minutes, take time to enjoy all that it offers.

GETTING THERE

In Mancos, head north on N. Main Street (State Highway 184) from Grand Avenue (US 160 business loop). Continue north for 0.5 mile (0.8 km) and turn right onto County Road 42. At 3 miles (4.8 km), turn left to stay on CR 42. Continue for 2.2 miles (3.5 km) to the San Juan National Forest boundary, where the road becomes Forest Road 561; follow it for 4.5 miles (7.2 km). Turn right onto FR 565, the road to Transfer Campground, and continue for 0.25 mile (0.4 km) to the trailhead.

ON THE TRAIL

Beginning from the Transfer Campground parking lot in the San Juan National Forest, look for the wooden sign designating the Big Al Trail, open only to foot traffic. The Mancos Spur Trail also begins here, so be sure to head out on the correct trail.

From the beginning, vegetation and trees swallow you. At about 155 feet (47 m), on the right, take some time to learn about Al Lorentzen, the trail's namesake. You will probably hear cows on the trail from almost the start. Livestock fencing begins to appear at times on both sides of the trail. Cow fences keep the cattle out, but plenty of animals scurry or fly about, from chipmunks and squirrels to Steller's jays and mule deer.

At a little over 0.1 mile (0.2 km), the trail crosses a wide bridge. Interpretive signage begins, with informational text on mule deer, the term "quaking aspen," and porcupines. According to the signs, beavers are also known to enjoy the habitat.

Another bench and bridge appear at a bit past 0.25 mile (0.4 km). As you weave through groves of aspens, little

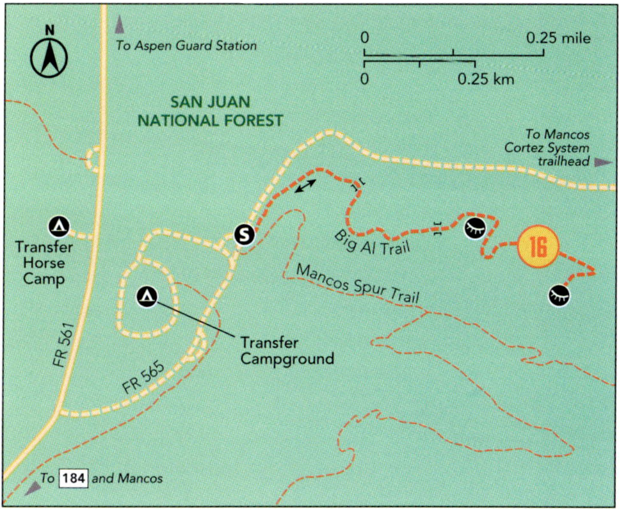

The Mancos River valley can be seen from the viewpoint.

openings are alive with wildflowers in season. Purple American vetch, mule's ears, and prairie thermopsis are just a few of the vibrant-colored flowers you can see.

At a little beyond 0.3 mile (0.5 km), find a bench with a viewpoint. If you are wowed by the view here, just wait until you reach the trail's end and the big overlook. The sound of the Mancos River below and quaking aspen around you, along with the sun on your face and the smells of the forest, provide a full sensory experience.

At about 0.4 mile (0.6 km), a sign warns about black bears, which can be found in the area but sightings are rare. The trail bends at almost 0.5 mile (0.8 km). Here it is vibrant with color from mule's ears, Indian paintbrush, and lupines. In the fall, the aspens blaze in gold.

Through some Gambel oak, the trail ends at an obvious overlook at 0.6 mile (1 km). Several benches allow you to rest, or you can walk from left to right along the fenced-off overlook to take in the views. Mount Hesperus dominates the landscape, along with the La Plata Mountains and the West Mancos River valley. Depending on the vegetation, you may also be able to see the Mancos River below.

As you follow the trail back to the start, be sure to stop and read any interpretive signs you missed on the way to the overlook. Enjoy the stroll back to the trailhead, taking in all the sights and sounds.

17 SHARKSTOOTH PASS

Distance: 3 miles (5 km)
Elevation gain: 1035 feet (320 m)
High point: 11,945 feet (3640 m)
Difficulty: Moderate
Trail surface: Dirt, rocks
Map: Trails Illustrated Durango Cortez
GPS: 38.8410538°N, 109.517134°W
Note: Leashed dogs allowed; no restroom or water access

> This high-altitude hike, part of the Mancos Spur, is a segment of the National Recreation Highline Loop that showcases the best of the San Juan Mountains views but doesn't take all day. You need a high-clearance vehicle to reach this trailhead. The hike is best June through September, though snow is possible through late June and in late September. Get out early in summer to avoid afternoon thunderstorms.

GETTING THERE

In Mancos, head north on N. Main Street (State Highway 184) from Grand Avenue (US 160 business loop). Continue

Take in the expansive vista from Sharkstooth Pass.

north for 0.5 mile (0.8 km) and turn right onto County Road 42. At 3 miles (4.8 km), turn left to stay on CR 42. Continue for 3.2 miles (5.1 km) to the San Juan National Forest boundary, where the road becomes Forest Road 561; follow it for 4.5 miles (7.2 km) to the junction with FR 565, the road to Transfer Campground. At this junction, stay left to continue north on FR 561. In about 0.75 mile (1.2 km), at the fork with FR 560, stay right to continue on FR 561.

In a little over 1 mile (1.6 km), at the T intersection where FR 561 ends, turn right onto FR 350 and follow it about 1.25 miles (2 km) to where FR 346 heads right. If recent weather makes it difficult to reach the trailhead, an option is to park at this split from FR 350, the point where FR 346 gets extremely rocky and rutted, and hike the 1.5 miles (2.4 km) to the trailhead. If FR 346 is passable, turn right onto it and follow it to its end at the trailhead.

ON THE TRAIL

From the road-end parking lot, take the Sharkstooth Trail to the left as it heads southeast and begins to climb (the trail to the right is the West Mancos Trail). A large scree field comes up on the left-hand side, ending in around 0.1 mile (0.2 km). You may hear the first squeaks from the happy marmots that live on the pass. Hespersus Mountain, a highlight of the San Juan National Forest, is in the background for most of this hike, evident as you begin to climb. The trail is quite rocky, and several downed trees line the path as it continues upward through fir and Engelmann spruce.

At 0.25 mile (0.4 km), you come upon another scree field. An abundance of rocks that still make up the trail shows that the scree once crossed over the path. As the trail returns to the spruce and fir forest, roots pop up along the path. Keep your feet about you to avoid tripping. Beautiful green mosses spread across the rock as you travel in and out of the shade.

At just shy of 0.5 mile (0.8 km), the trail begins to roll a bit, easing the climb, while a potential stream crossing greets you after this point. A bigger water crossing occurs in about 250 feet (76 m), with the soothing sounds of trickling little falls and birds happily chirping. The trail begins to climb, with the water continuing right below you. Wildflowers add color, from yarrow to old-man-of-the-mountain.

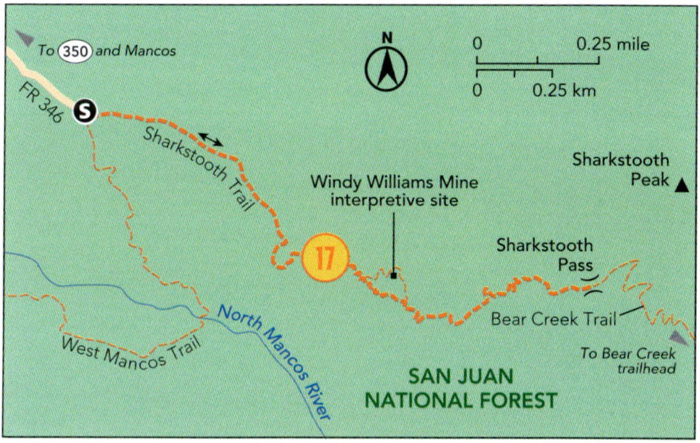

The trail switchbacks as it gains elevation, winding so the water that was once on the right-hand side is now on the left. A trickle of water across some scree may greet you at 0.7 mile (1.1 km)—the water level may be higher, depending on recent weather and time of year.

A fairytale-like waterfall covered in moss on the right could form icicles in October. Recent overnight temperatures and snow are often the first signs that winter is coming. Some color might still exist, even if many of the autumn hues are battened down or whisked away with early snow. Elderberries and mushrooms found all along this part of the woodsy trail are a sure sign of autumn.

At a water crossing at 0.75 mile (1.2 km), use either a rock or log path to cross without getting wet feet. This is a tributary of the North Mancos River. Look for a wide-open view of Hesperus Mountain as the trail continues to switchback.

At 1 mile (1.6 km), a side trail on the left leads to the Windy Williams Mine site (see Going Farther, below). Beyond this side trail, the main path encounters several more views of Hesperus Mountain, the tallest peak in the La Platas at 13,232 feet (4033 m). The switchbacks continue as the trail begins to open up and heads more southeast, leaving the Hesperus Mountain views behind for scree and views of Centennial Peak.

At 1.3 miles (2 km), a fragile tundra sign on the right is a good reminder to follow Leave No Trace principles. Now above the tree line, the trail continues to climb as the landmark that gives the trail its name comes into view: Sharkstooth Pass, the saddle between Sharkstooth and Centennial Peaks. The highest of the freestanding Cathedral Spires, Sharkstooth sits at 12,630 feet (3767 m). Centennial and Sharkstooth Peaks are popular with mountaineers, so you may see climbers attempting the summits. You might spot a mountain biker as well, although they have to hike the bike in places.

Along the trail, you can see the shark's tooth for which the pass is named.

In between scree and the trail, fields of wildflowers including Indian paintbrush and columbines add color to the rocky terrain. Other hikers mentioned mountain bell-wort and asters. The tunes of songbirds are now replaced by the sounds of curious pikas and marmots. Pikas talk with squeaky-toy sounds, while marmots sound more like a high-pitched fire alarm battery waking you up in the middle of the night.

The trail becomes loose as it switchbacks up. A sign once designated the top of the pass, with directional arrows pointing west for Sharkstooth trailhead in 1.8 miles (2.9 km) and Bear Creek trailhead in 1.7 miles (2.7 km), but at the time of publication, the pass was marked only by a large rock cairn. The 360-degree views are worth the effort to get here. Look east for the La Plata Range and west for Mesa Verde National Park and the town of Cortez. If the clouds cooperate, look north to see if there is a view toward Telluride.

Fuel up and then start the trek back down to the trailhead. Your view now looks more to the west, with Hesperus Mountain on your left. As you leave the scree fields behind, the chatter from marmots and pikas soon ends as you enter spruce and fir forest while switching back down the trail. If you didn't take the side trail for the interpretive loop to the Windy Williams Mine site on the way up, check it out on the return trip to the trailhead.

GOING FARTHER

The side trail to the north of the Sharkstooth Trail is a 0.5-mile (0.8 km) loop around the area of the Windy Williams Mine interpretive site. You can see metal, remnants of old mining equipment, and lumber. Signs along this trail explain the small mining operation and the remains of a waterwheel that was used to crush ore. If you skip the mining trail on the way up, you can enjoy it on the way back down.

If you would like a full-day hike, you can continue down from Sharkstooth Pass on the not-quite 3.2-mile (5.1 km) Bear Creek Trail, which terminates at about 4.6 miles (7.4 km) from the Sharkstooth trailhead. Similar to the Sharkstooth Trail, the Bear Creek Trail is dirt with rocks, wide in some spots and narrow in others. The descent and ascent back are a bit steeper than the Sharkstooth Trail to Sharkstooth Pass. At the Bear Creek trailhead, turn around to head back the way you came, for a total of 9.3 miles (15 km).

The Rampart Hills are a dramatic feature of this hike.

18 RAMPARTS LOOP

Distance: 5.4 miles (8.7 km)
Elevation gain: 1079 feet (329 m)
High point: 9344 feet (2848 m)
Difficulty: Moderate
Trail surface: Dirt, rocks
Map: Trails Illustrated Durango Cortez
GPS: 37.3904815°N, 108.3260784°W
Note: Leashed dogs allowed; no restrooms or water access

> The Ramparts Loop highlights the Rampart Hills, an igneous rock outcrop in the Echo Basin area of the San Juan Mountains. The trail's steeper and often rocky descents and ascents require strong knees and ankles. This multiuse trail is open to dirt bikes, mountain bikes, and horses; in the fall, it is also open to elk hunting (archery). This hike is best May through October, with the potential to snowshoe it in winter.

GETTING THERE

From Mancos, take US 160 east for 3 miles (5 km). Turn left onto Echo Basin Road (County Road 44). Follow the road for 6.8 miles (11 km); the road becomes Forest Road 566 when the pavement ends at the junction with CR M. In a little over 0.5 mile (0.8 km) from the pavement end, FR 566 makes a sharp right turn past Weber Reservoir. In another 6.3 miles (10.1 km), make a slight left onto FR 331. From the turn onto FR 331, the T-Down corral and campground parking are 0.1 mile (0.2 km) farther.

ON THE TRAIL

In the heart of the San Juan National Forest, this trail can be hiked in either direction. This description heads clockwise. Look for a brown trail sign across the road from the corral to begin. (To hike the trail counterclockwise, continue north from the corral to a turnoff for a parking lot and primitive campsite on the left; head up that road and find the trail on the right-hand side.)

From the very beginning of this hike, your senses will be intrigued. It doesn't take long before you hear the buzz of bees, see the flash of butterflies across the landscape, and hear the sound of birds. Hummingbirds flutter among a variety of wildflowers. Bears, snakes, and deer are some of the more common animals seen here. You might see a baby whipsnake crossing the trail. Or you might hear cracking sounds and suddenly see deer springing across the trail ahead of you—a reminder that you are just a visitor to their home.

Good shade greets you almost from the start, a mix of aspen and pine. The narrow and off-camber singletrack begins to head downhill. At 0.5 mile (0.8 km), there is a cow gate. Remember: if you find a gate open, leave it open; if you find one closed, close it after you walk through.

The singletrack trail heads toward the Rampart Hills.

Enjoy the view of the scenic Rampart Hills.

The trail then bends, with views of Mesa Verde National Park and Mancos State Park to the southwest. As the trail continues downhill, a short time later it leads back into the quaking aspens as the downhill becomes looser and steeper.

At 1 mile (1.6 km), you can hear the trickle of water on the right, depending on the time of year. A potential easy water crossing follows. As the trail climbs, views of the igneous rocks that make up Rampart Hills can be seen on the right. The birds continue to serenade and various wildflowers including columbine and lupine line the trail. The route winds through aspens and Gambel oak.

Just past 2.5 miles (4 km), the trail ends at a road. Go right and follow the road southeast to continue clockwise. There is limited shade here, so drink some water.

At 2.8 miles (4.5 km), a trail to the right heads west along the ridgetop; continue straight ahead. There are views again of the hills on the right. Tall western groundswell, columbine, and pinecones larger than a fist dot the landscape.

You encounter a washed-out road at 2.9 miles (4.6 km). A trail sign on the right indicates it is time to leave the road and turn right to head back up on the singletrack. On the left might be a seasonal pool of water perfect for dunking your hat before you begin climbing.

Catch your breath and take in the view of Rampart Hills on the left. The trail gets steeper and looser. In the spring, it can be overgrown and washed out in spots. A larger seasonal water crossing at 3.5 miles (5.6 km) may mean some wet feet.

A short distance later, the Rampart Hills come into view again. Enjoy a water break and look back, where Mesa Verde and Mancos State Park can be seen through the oaks. Two more potential water crossings occur at 3.9 and 4.1 miles (6.2 and 6.6 km). As the trail switchbacks, down trees and debris may be a hazard in the area, making the trail slippery in spots. Enjoy the false hellebores growing alongside the trail. Birds chirp while bees and hummingbirds enjoy the wildflowers blooming.

At 4.2 miles (6.8 km), you may need to open a cow gate. Cattle also roam the hillsides, and hikers have reported having to bushwack to avoid them. The trail continues a nice meander through the forest with the stream to the right. The pines mix with the aspens as you move closer to the trailhead.

A large water crossing at 5.2 miles (8.3 km) is the last challenge before you hit the primitive campsite road at 5.4 miles (8.6 km). Follow the road down to the corral if that is where you parked your vehicle.

CORTEZ

Located in the southwest corner of Colorado, the town of Cortez is a gateway to canyon country and desert to the west and south, as well as to the San Juan Mountains to the east and north. Cortez, at the junction of US 160 and US 491, is 25 miles (40 km) from the Four Corners area and is the closest town to Mesa Verde National Park from the west. The seat of Montezuma County, Cortez has many options for food and lodging as a base for exploring the region. From San Juan National Forest to Bureau of Land Management sites, Montezuma County is 76 percent public lands, with mountain biking a prime attraction.

19 HAWKINS PRESERVE LOOP

Distance: 3 miles (5 km), plus observing the pueblo
Elevation gain: 112 feet (34 m)
High point: 6100 feet (1859 m)
Difficulty: Easy
Trail surface: Dirt, stones, slickrock
Map: Trails Illustrated Durango Cortez
GPS: 37.3494121°N, 108.4978521°W
Note: Leashed dogs allowed; pit toilets on trails; no water access

OPPOSITE: *Art installation along the trail in Hawkins Preserve*

McElmo Canyon serves as the background for most of the hike.

With land donated by Jack Hawkins in the 1990s, Cortez Cultural Center opened 122-acre (49-hectare) Hawkins Preserve in 2004 as a conservation easement held by Montezuma Land Conservancy. The archaeological and natural resources once inhabited by the Ancestral Puebloans are now protected. The preserve, free to visit, is open year-round from sunup to sundown, and the trails can be snowshoed in winter. You can find pockets of shade, but it is exposed in many areas.

GETTING THERE

In the town of Cortez, head west on US 160 (W. Main Street) toward S. Chestnut Street for 0.2 mile (0.3 km). Turn left onto S. Maple Street for 0.3 mile (0.4 km). Turn right onto W. Fourth Street, then make a quick left onto S. Oak Street. Follow it south for 0.6 mile (0.9 km) and turn right onto Verde Vu Drive. After a little over 0.1 mile (0.2 km), turn left onto S. Cedar Street. In 0.1 mile (0.2 km) the parking area is on the right.

ON THE TRAIL

There are several ways to enjoy the trails at Hawkins Preserve and different routes to take. This hike includes most of the preserve's highlights, including the Hawkins Pueblo and Patrick's Point. Take a moment to read the literature at the kiosk near the start of the preserve to learn more about this culturally significant area.

From the South Cedar Street parking lot, begin heading west on the multiuse paved Mesa View Trail, popular with walkers and bikers. Shortly, pass the Slickrock Trail to the left and at a bit over 0.1 mile (0.2 km), pass the Runs Road Trail to

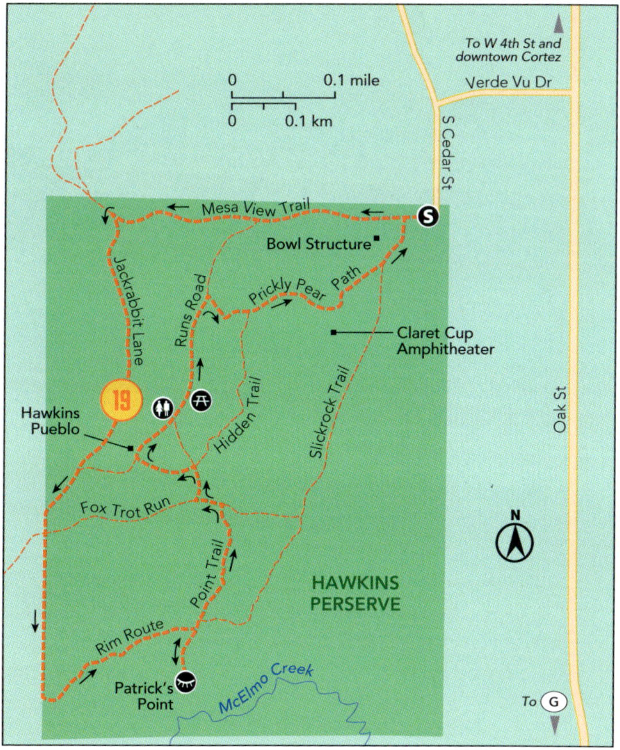

A structure protects the Hawkins Pueblo from further erosion.

the left. At about 0.3 mile (0.4 km), turn left onto Jackrabbit Lane and follow the typically hard-packed red dirt trail heading south. Be on the lookout for waste rock that has fallen from pueblos and other structures.

Piñon pine and cactus dot the landscape, along with sagebrush and juniper. Lizards dart across the trail. Continue south until the trail ends at about 0.7 mile (1.1 km). Turn left onto Rim Route and follow it east 0.2 mile (0.3 km). Along the Rim Route, you can see McElmo Canyon, the La Plata

Mountains, and Mesa Verde National Park. You may also be able to see rock climbers along this route. If you are a climber, you may apply for a permit to climb in the area. There is great bouldering to be found in McElmo Canyon as well as additional sites under the rim. The Hawkins Fire in May 2021 burned much of the vegetation below the upper ridge and the bench in the McElmo Canyon area of the preserve.

At about 0.9 mile (1.4 km), take a right onto the Point Trail and follow it about 100 feet (30 m) to Patrick's Point. Enjoy a break on the log benches at the point, taking in water and maybe a snack with the view. The Dakota Sandstone cliffs offer a home to many animals and lizards.

Retrace your steps back to the junction with the Rim Route and cross it to hike about 100 feet (30 m) on the slickrock Point Trail until you reach Fox Trot Run. Turn left onto Fox Trot Run and in 0.1 mile (0.2 km) from the Rim Route you come upon the Hawkins Pueblo, protected from above from rain and snow, at about 1 mile (1.6 km) from the trailhead.

The pueblo was the site of looting and pot hunting over hundreds of years before it was protected. Walk around the pueblo to get a view from all sides, including the middens and kiva depressions. A habitation room block and mounds can still be seen. You may see a rubble pile south of the pueblo, further evidence of life in the area.

When you have marveled at the craftsmanship, head north onto Runs Road. At the intersection with the Point Trail are pit toilets with fun names—Lizard Lounge and Robin's Nest. Just north of the toilets is the Wyatt Picnic Area, approximately 0.2 mile (0.3 km) from the site. Turn to the right onto Prickly Pear Path. You can guess what you may see along this path! As you walk among the cactus, look right to see the Claret Cup Amphitheater, named after the state cactus. Continue east on Prickly Pear Path, which meanders a little over 0.2 mile (0.3 km) before joining the Slickrock Trail at about 1.4 miles (2.2 km) from the trailhead. Turn left onto the Slickrock Trail.

As you travel about 200 feet (61 m) on this trail, on the left you will see the Bowl Structure. Made to represent a decorated pottery bowl common to the Ancestral Puebloans, it is buried in sand. As a way to showcase local art, the Cortez Cultural Center has established the Art on the Trail initiative, and the Bowl Structure is part of that effort.

At the Mesa View Trail, turn right and in about 100 feet (30 m) you will be back at the trailhead.

20 TRUST AND HIPPIE HOUSE LOOP

Distance: 6.2 miles (9.9 km)
Elevation gain: 320 feet (97.5 m)
High point: 6425 feet (1958 m)
Difficulty: Moderate
Trail surface: Dirt, stones, roots, slickrock
Map: Trails Illustrated Durango Cortez
GPS: 37.3494121°N, 108.4978521°W
Note: Leashed dogs allowed; seasonal portable toilet at trailhead; no water access

> The Trust and Hippie House Loops are in the 27-mile (43 km) Phil's World trail system, part of the Bureau of Land Management's "Backyard to Backcountry" program. Phil Vigil came to the Four Corners area in the late 1980s and created his own bike routes, including on BLM land where Phil's World trails exist today. The best time to hike the trail is May through October; there is little shade. It can be snowshoed in winter.

GETTING THERE

From the town of Cortez on US 160 (W. Main Street), head east from S. Market Street for 8.3 miles (13 km), passing the

This loop is open to hiking and mountain biking.

road to the right for Montezuma County Fairgrounds, and exit at the next road to the right. Make a U-turn and follow US 160 west for 3.3 miles (5 km). Turn right onto Road 30.1 (a little west of the road to the fairgrounds). Follow Road 30.1 about 0.2 mile (0.3 km) to the turnoff into the parking lot.

ON THE TRAIL

On the east side of the parking lot, a BLM sign denotes the beginning of the Trust Loop. Follow this directional trail clockwise. Maps and signs along the trail help keep you heading in the right direction. Keep your eyes and ears open, as this trail is open to bikes and horses. At 0.3 mile (0.5 km), you reach the first trail junction, with a sign and map. Go straight as the trail heads downhill, going in and out of scrub brush with little to no shade.

At 0.5 mile (0.8 km), the trail heads downhill again and crosses a bridge over McElmo Creek. Mesa Verde deer, rodents, and even bats are common in the area. Golden eagles roost within a protected area nearby, so you may be treated to some birds of prey circling for food overhead. Sagebrush lizards may cross your path. Snakes are also

Directional signs help keep you on the right trail.

common, including midget faded rattlesnakes and striped whipsnakes—even more reason to stay on the trail.

At approximately 1 mile (1.6 km), a hill takes you up to a good lookout spot for Sleeping Ute Mountain to the west. You can find bits of shade in this section. On the left at about 1.3 miles (2 km), you will see a rock tower warning about falling rocks. Shepherds once used these towers as a warning about a boundary or approaching a cliff.

The trail reaches another junction at 1.6 miles (2.6 km); head left to continue onto the Hippie House Loop. (If you want to shorten your hike, you can make a sharp right to head back on the Trust Loop to the parking lot.)

As you weave through the pines and scrub brush, look east as Mesa Verde National Park comes into view at around 2.8 miles (4.5 km). The UNESCO World Heritage site stays in view for the next mile as the trail meanders. Can you spot the rusted coffee can hanging from a tree on the right-hand side?

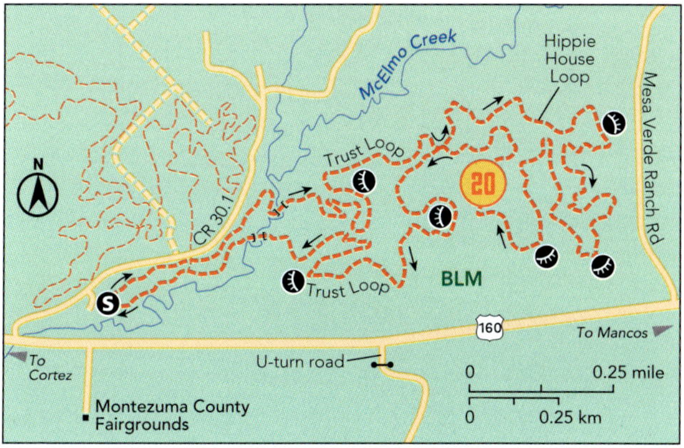

A banked downhill just after 4 miles (6.4 km) is steep but manageable. The trail begins to open up. Road noise may be heard as views of US 160 can be seen from the trail. At 4.6 miles (7.4 km), the trail reaches the junction with the Trust Loop. Stay to the left to get back onto the Trust Loop heading west toward the trailhead.

At 5 miles (8 km), after a hill you once again see the tower of stacked rocks. Sleeping Ute Mountain is once again in the background to the west. As you continue, you can see the other side of the Trust Loop that took you east to begin the hike.

At 5.8 miles (9.3 km), cross another bridge over the creek. Continuing along the mesa top, at about 6 miles (9.7 km) pass the trail to the first junction on the start of the Trust Loop. Soon you reach the trailhead.

DOLORES

The small town of Dolores, on State Route 145 about 12 miles (19 km) north of Cortez, stretches between the Dolores River to the south and cliffs to the north. Tubing, swimming, and fishing are popular along this river. Don't be surprised to see people carrying a kayak to a put-in spot or an angler trying to catch brook, brown, or rainbow trout on the river.

Located at the mouth of McPhee Reservoir, Dolores has lodging and dining options and is home to the Canyons of the Ancients Museum and Visitors Center. Two of this chapter's hikes begin in the town's west end; the third is about 35 miles (56 km) to the northwest along the West Dolores River.

21 DOLORES RIVER TRAIL

Distance: 2.9 miles (4.6 km)
Elevation gain: 29 feet (8.8 m)
High point: 6936 feet (2114 m)
Difficulty: Easy
Trail surface: Gravel, dirt, pavement
Map: Trails Illustrated Durango Cortez
GPS: 37.4709°N, 108.5176°W
Note: Leashed dogs allowed; seasonal portable toilet at trailhead, restrooms at Joe Rowell Park, restrooms and water access at library

OPPOSITE: *The hike to Geyser Springs (Hike 23) begins by crossing the West Dolores River.*

Along the Dolores River Trail in 2016, local fourth-graders created an art installation of nine planet displays, including dwarf planet Pluto, spacing them apart according to scale. You can start from either end: McPhee Reservoir parking lot for McPhee Overlook Trail (Hike 22) or Dolores Library. The best times to enjoy this hike are April through October, but it is also accessible in winter. A lack of shade makes this trail better for mornings or evenings.

GETTING THERE

From State Highway 145 in Dolores, turn north onto B Street. Very quickly you reach Central Avenue; turn left (west). Continue on as the street becomes County Road 28. In 0.2 mile (0.3 km), keep left to stay on CR 28. The road ends in about 0.25 mile (0.4 km) at a parking area and trailhead for the Dolores River Trail and the McPhee Overlook Trail (Hike 22).

ON THE TRAIL

This hike begins at the west end of the trail, from the parking lot for the McPhee Overlook Trail (Hike 22). Across the

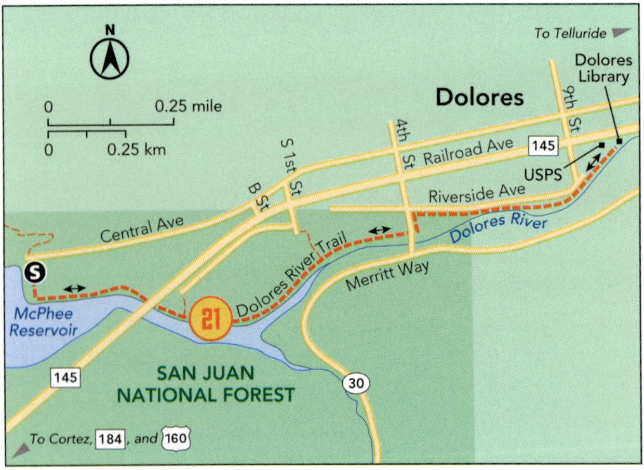

After you pass under the highway bridge, you leave the sound of traffic behind.

parking lot from the cliffs, a sign designates the start of the Dolores River Trail. The path is wide open as it heads south toward the river; in 0.1 mile (0.2 km), it begins to bend east, where a bench is a good place to enjoy the view.

Yarrow and rubber rabbitbrush line the sides of the trail as it passes under the Highway 145 bridge at around 0.3 mile (0.5 km). The trail crosses a berm that provides protection from flooding of the Dolores River.

Have you found the first planet sign yet? Most signs are on the right as you head upstream. The students created the entire piece, from concept and presentation to design and installation. On the left-hand side, Joe Rowell Park is at the 0.4-mile (0.6 km) mark. You may see kids playing in the park or hear a ball game or soccer game in progress.

Access to the river begins at this same point, designated by signs on the right. A metal sign with hooks also denotes areas good for fishing along the public areas of the Dolores River. You now begin to hear less road noise and more sounds of the river. Park access opens up on the left at about 0.7 mile (1.1 km). River access points continue as you

Admire the colorful cottonwoods along the Dolores River Trail in fall.

head along the trail—on a hot day you might want to take a plunge in the river to cool off.

At 0.9 mile (1.4 km), the trail comes to a T junction with South Fourth Street. A sign for the trail has a good reminder of the Leave No Trace principles: "This is the water we drink." Turn left onto the sidewalk and keep an eye out for a planet sign on the left as you head north.

Follow the sidewalk to Riverside Avenue; turn right onto Riverside and follow the road. The nondesignated trail picks back up on the right-hand side after the 1-mile (1.6 km) mark, so keep your eyes open. Planet signs continue, including Saturn and Neptune, as you follow the Dolores River.

At about 1.4 miles (2.2 km), the trail terminates right after the Dolores Post Office, near the Dolores Public Library. If you have some backpack space, stop by the free book area at the front of the library to find a few gems to bring back with you.

In the fall, you may enjoy a wild apple from one of the trees that line the river close to the library. Near the library are brain-building activity suggestions—fun to read about. These ideas, from playing the listening game and taking a seasonal stroll, are all suggestions that children and adults can participate in to enhance their hike.

Were you able to find all nine planet signs along the way to the library? If not, try to complete the challenge on the way back as you retrace your steps to the McPhee Overlook trailhead. Play the color game—one of the brain-building suggestions—or just enjoy the sights and sounds as you meander along downstream.

22 MCPHEE OVERLOOK

Distance: 12 miles (19 km)
Elevation gain: 1400 feet (426 m)
High point: 7230 feet (2203 m)
Difficulty: Challenging
Trail surface: Dirt, roots, rocks
Map: Trails Illustrated Durango Cortez
GPS: 37.4712373°N, 108.520404°W
Note: Leashed dogs allowed (some areas designated off-leash); seasonal portable toilet at trailhead, restrooms and water access at House Creek Campground

> McPhee Reservoir, open to fishing, boating, and paddling, is fed by the Dolores River. The out-and-back hike along the McPhee Overlook Trail can be lengthened or shortened, but as described below, it turns around at House Creek Campground. The best times for this hike are May through October; the trail is closed seasonally to protect winter habitat for elk and deer. A lack of shade makes this hike better for mornings or evenings.

GETTING THERE

From State Highway 145 in Dolores, turn north onto B Street. Very quickly you reach Central Avenue; turn left

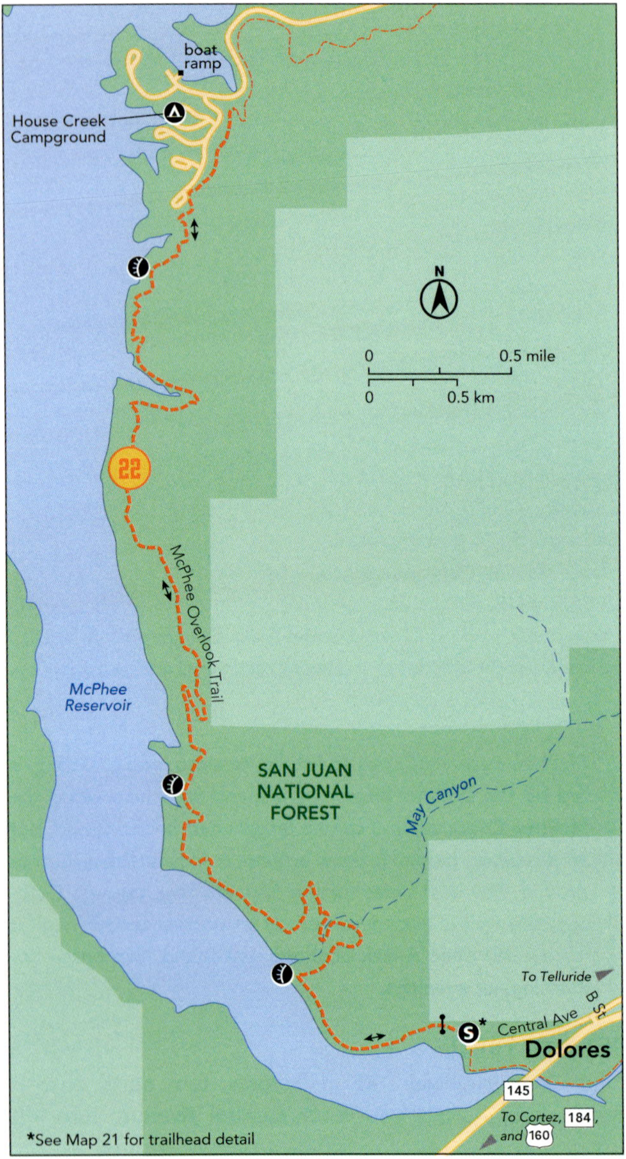
boat ramp
House Creek Campground
N
0
0.5 mile
0
0.5 km
22
McPhee Overlook Trail
McPhee Reservoir
SAN JUAN NATIONAL FOREST
May Canyon
To Telluride
B St
Central Ave
S*
Dolores
145
To Cortez, 184, and 160
*See Map 21 for trailhead detail

(west). Continue on as the street becomes County Road 28. In 0.2 mile (0.3 km), keep left to stay on CR 28. The road ends in about 0.25 mile (0.4 km) at a parking area and trailhead for the McPhee Overlook Trail and the Dolores River Trail (Hike 21).

ON THE TRAIL

A historic cemetery is to the left of the trailhead. This multiuse trail is shared with mountain bikers and horses. Please note: To protect elk and deer habitat in winter, the 1-mile (1.6 km) section of trail from Dolores to May Canyon is closed from December 1 to April 15, and the section from May Canyon to House Creek Campground is closed from December 1 to May 1.

Begin by ascending on several switchbacks as the trail quickly climbs 115 feet (35 m). Leveling off a bit, you pass several cool rock features at about 0.2 mile (0.3 km). The rocks disappear as the trail heads into a pine forest. At a bit past 0.25 mile (0.4 km), you come upon a cattle and bike gate. Pass through the gate, leaving it as you found it.

The trail now hugs the reservoir, the second-largest in the state and the largest in San Juan National Forest, with 50 miles (80 km) of shoreline that includes juniper, sagebrush, and piñon pines. Depending on the time of year, the reservoir water levels may be very low.

Make your way across the dirt terrain on the undulating trail. Rocks and roots are obstacles found throughout the hike. At times, you may think the trail will drop over the edge as it heads toward May Canyon. As it meanders through the forest, the smell of pine is strong. Butterflies sail between the flowering cactus and columbines. Piñon jays and Steller's jays may serenade you as you walk. You can see why elk and deer choose such a dense forest for a winter habitat. As the Dolores River dumps into the reservoir, you can often hear the waterway spill.

Shy of 1 mile (1.6 km), you come to an overlook on the left—one of the best—as the trail enters May Canyon. Now heading northeast, the trail bends away from the reservoir to get across the canyon. As you descend into the canyon, the trail begins to change and you reach the canyon bottom at 1.2 miles (1.9 km).

Depending on recent weather and time of year, there may be a water crossing at 1.4 miles (2.2 km). Following the trail as it bends around the canyon, you may notice the winter trail closing sign. Before climbing out of the canyon, you can access the reservoir to take a quick dip.

The trail climbs and switchbacks toward a meadow. It is steeper than the first one, coming in at close to a 16 percent grade. As you enter the meadow area filled with grasses at 1.5 miles (2.4 km), you will see numerous cow paths. You may actually find cows grazing in the area, typically from May until the end of July. Help the ranchers out by leaving gates as you find them.

As you make your way through the green and yellowish grasses, a lone tree stands within the meadow. I checked my photo of it on the Seek app (see Appendix A: Resources), which indicated this is a stone pine, a rarity in the United States except in California. It would be fitting if it is one, since it stands on its own in the meadow.

The trail begins to flatten out at this point. Drink some water if you haven't been doing so already, as a view of Sleeping Ute Mountain fills the background to the west. Expect this area to be buggy, especially with grasshoppers. If you aren't dodging cow pies, you will be dodging the grasshoppers as they zigzag along the path. Homes appear on the opposite side of the reservoir. As you continue, reservoir views appear again at around 1.9 miles (3 km).

At just past 2 miles (3.2 km), the trail leaves the meadow behind and hugs the reservoir again. Pines, juniper, and scrub brush dot the sides of the trail. This part resembles

A lone stone pine makes for a dramatic landmark on the trail.

much of the beginning mile with a few areas of slickrock to maneuver. As the trail heads back into San Juan National Forest, you can tell why it is known as a birding hot spot, with kestrels and sparrows, meadowlarks and northern flickers.

This trail was built from grants, including from the Great Outdoors of Colorado, to add an additional multiuse trail in the Boggy Draw Trail System. The trail was begun in 2014 and built in phases until it was completed in 2017. The labor for the trail was a true collaboration between the Mesa Verde Backcountry Horsemen, Southwest Conservation Corps, the National Forest Foundation, and the Southwest Colorado Cycling Association. From the easement on private property to the retaining walls helping to keep the beginning of the trail from eroding, it was created with conservation in mind for generations of outdoor enthusiasts to enjoy. It was granted the Conservation Legacy Award in 2018 for the collaborative effort.

At around 3.5 miles (5.6 km), continue on toward House Creek Campground; a friendly horned lizard might hang out next to the trail. Rattlesnakes have commonly been reported on the trail, so be careful if you step off the trail to allow

Wildflowers are abundant on the McPhee Overlook Trail.

horses or bikers to pass. There are also a lot of cacti just ready to prick you. Keep drinking water as the path heads in and out of the shade.

The trail continues to hug the reservoir, always on your left. At points the vegetation is thicker and you may lose sight of the water. Rest assured: the trail curves and the water will come back into view.

At just shy of 5 miles (8 km) is another spectacular lookout. From this vantage point, you can see the main McPhee

Recreation Area, including the boat ramp and campground. Before you reach the campground, another overlook has a view of the water crashing on the rocks below. You may be able to see Goodman Point and the Blue Mountains in Utah by looking west on clear enough days.

At approximately 6 miles (9.6 km) sits House Creek Campground, 500 feet (152 m) below this turnaround point. House Creek dumps into the reservoir just north of the campground, where the trail begins to turn northeast to follow the creek upstream. On a hot day, it's a good idea to head down to the campground area to cool off in the water, use the restroom, or at least fill up on water!

For this hike, turn around above the campground to begin the 6-mile (9.6 km) trek back to the trailhead. Even though you are covering the same miles, your reservoir views are different as you look toward the Dolores River spillway. It is hard to believe that the logging towns of Big Bend, abandoned in 1891, and McPhee, abandoned after a mill fire in 1948, were once located where the McPhee Dam now stands.

It is nice to find a gem of a trail that offers a different look and scenery like this trail does. "Lonesome Tree," as it could be called, takes on a new look as you cross the meadow. A grasshopper attack is still imminent on the way back. Depending on the season, applying some bug spray may help on your return to the Dolores trailhead.

GOING FARTHER

From House Creek Campground, you can continue on the McPhee Overlook Trail an additional 3 miles (4.8 km) to the trail's end at Bean Canyon, 6 additional miles (9.6 km) total, for the complete 18-mile (29 km) out-and-back. You can also hike the complete 9-mile (14.5 km) trail one-way as a shuttle hike, leaving a second car at the trailhead for Forest Trail 199—Boggy Trail.

23 GEYSER SPRING

Distance: 3 miles (5 km)
Elevation gain: 500 feet (152 m)
High point: 9100 feet (2773 m)
Difficulty: Easy to moderate
Trail surface: Dirt
Map: Trails Illustrated Durango Cortez
GPS: 37.75728°N, 108.12813°W
Note: Leashed dogs allowed; no restroom or water access

> This hike takes you deep into the San Juan Mountains to the only true geyser in Colorado. Oxygen is displaced at the geyser's surface by carbon dioxide and hydrogen sulfide—if you experience a headache or feel nauseated or lightheaded, leave the area immediately. You may encounter horseback riders or mountain bikers on this multiuse trail, but more likely you'll find very few others. This trail is best hiked spring through fall.

GETTING THERE

From the town of Dolores, head east on State Highway 145 for 12 miles (19 km). Turn left onto County Road 38 (Forest Road 535) and follow it for 23.3 miles (37 km). About 2 miles (3.2 km) south of the town of Dunton, the parking area for the Geyser Spring Trail is on the right.

ON THE TRAIL

From the trailhead parking lot, follow the trail across the footbridge over the West Dolores River. The hard-packed dirt trail starts to slowly climb as the aspens and pines begin to tower over you. Depending on the time of year, white and purple wildflowers may border the trail. The flowers are frequented by hummingbirds and butterflies.

Enjoy expansive views of the San Juans on the way to Geyser Spring.

Hikers may have a potential water crossing at 0.4 mile (0.6 km). After this crossing, the trail continues to climb. Keep your eyes open, as roots and rocks become a potential hazard on the trail as you make your way to the geyser.

At 0.7 mile (1.1 km), the trail flattens out a bit, and you may get your first smells of sulfur, depending on the wind direction. The trail begins to switchback as it climbs again. Indian paintbrush lines the trail and the sounds of quaking aspen are abundant if you hike the trail on a breezy day.

You can see some bubbling water on the right-hand side at 0.9 mile (1.4 km) and there's a strong smell of sulfur now. Restoration and trail damage may be seen in 200 feet (61 m). Areas of slide and trail damage may continue on the right-hand side as you continue toward the geyser. Another potential water crossing can be found about 300 feet (91 m) from the restoration area.

At 1.2 miles (1.9 km), you can hear the West Dolores River as you cross a ridge with views of the San Miguel Mountains. On the left at 1.25 miles (2 km), a sign designates that horses

Geyser Spring is the only true geyser in Colorado.

and bikes are no longer allowed on the trail: the sensitive area is open to foot travel only.

The trail passes through a fenced area and begins to travel downhill. The trail narrows now, is uneven, and features many hazards, including rocks and roots. Mining activity once occurred in the area. It is important to stay safely away from mining areas. After the descent, the trail clears to the right. Friendly Weidemeyer's admiral butterflies may treat you to a show as they fly from wildflower to wildflower. Catch a peekaboo view of the geyser through the pine trees on the right side at 1.3 miles (2.1 km).

At 1.5 miles (2.4 km), the bubbling green and blue geyser appears on your right. At a steady temperature of 82.4°F (28°C) year-round, the geyser erupts regularly—typically every half hour to forty-five minutes. However, the eruption is not much more than water trickling over the pool edges into Geyser Creek and some additional bubbling.

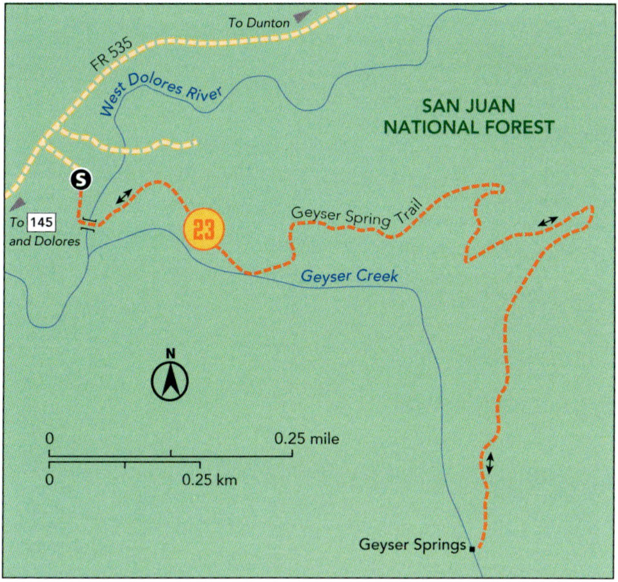

After enjoying this geological marvel, test your echo on the way back to the trailhead. The scenery is just as beautiful on the return, with continuous views of the San Miguel Range. As you follow the trail back toward the trailhead, pass by the slide areas and wildflowers for a second view. The trail opens back up to the valley again before you reach the bridge and trailhead parking lot.

OPPOSITE: *Corncob House is one of seven sites along the Sand Canyon Trail (Hike 27).*

PART 3: CANYONS OF THE ANCIENTS NATIONAL MONUMENT

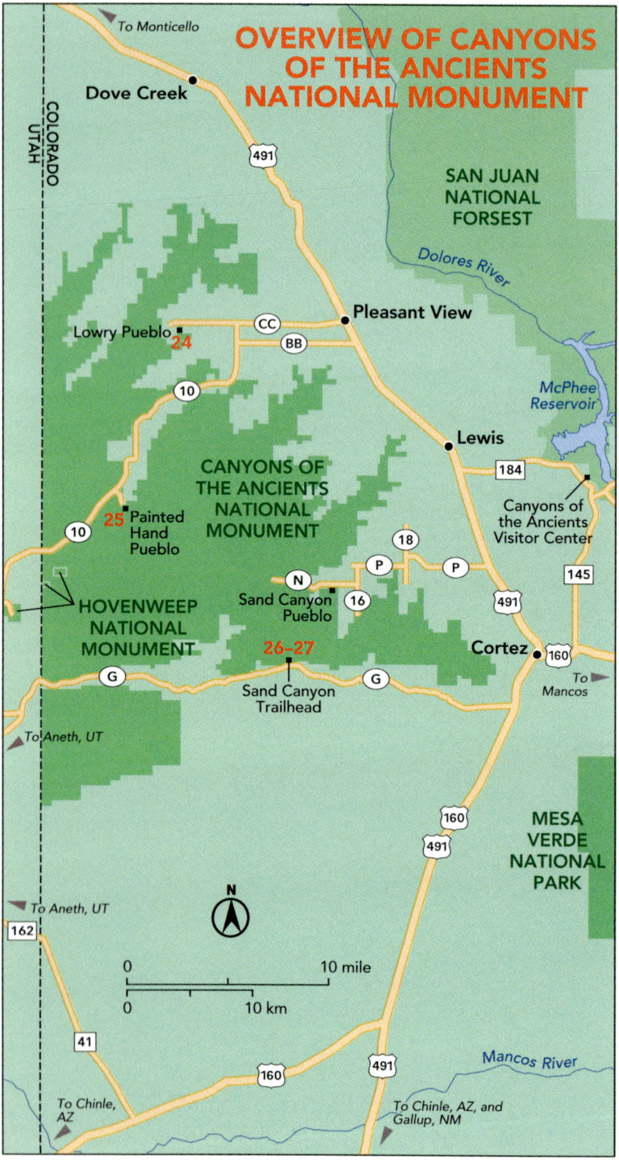

OVERVIEW OF CANYONS OF THE ANCIENTS NATIONAL MONUMENT
To Monticello
Dove Creek
COLORADO
UTAH
491
SAN JUAN NATIONAL FORSEST
Dolores River
Pleasant View
CC
BB
Lowry Pueblo
24
10
McPhee Reservoir
Lewis
184
CANYONS OF THE ANCIENTS NATIONAL MONUMENT
Canyons of the Ancients Visitor Center
25
Painted Hand Pueblo
18
P
N
16
145
Sand Canyon Pueblo
HOVENWEEP NATIONAL MONUMENT
26–27
Cortez
160
G
Sand Canyon Trailhead
To Mancos
To Aneth, UT
MESA VERDE NATIONAL PARK
N
To Aneth, UT
162
0
10 mile
0
10 km
41
Mancos River
To Chinle, AZ
To Chinle, AZ, and Gallup, NM

PLEASANT VIEW AREA

Canyons of the Ancients National Monument Visitor Center and Museum (formerly the Anasazi Heritage Center) are located on State Highway 184 just west of Dolores. The visitor center offers information, maps, and publications, with outdoor kiosks supplied with travel and hiking brochures when the center is closed. The museum features exhibits, a picnic area, and an outdoor 0.5-mile (0.8 km) one-way trail to Dominguez and Escalante Pueblos, occupied by Ancestral Puebloans in CE 1120s. The visitor center and museum are open Tuesday through Saturday from March through October, and Wednesday through Saturday November through February.

From the visitor center and museum, travelers to some of the monument's sites can head west on CO 184 to US 491 at Lewis, then turn either north to Pleasant View to access northern sites or south to Cortez to access southern sites. Pleasant View is an unincorporated community, so nearest options for food and lodging are in Dolores or Cortez. County roads heading west from Pleasant View lead to Lowry Pueblo (Hike 24) in Crow Canyon Wilderness Study Area and to Painted Hand Pueblo (Hike 25) deep in the monument near the Utah state line. From Painted Hand Pueblo, travelers can also continue on county roads to Hovenweep National Monument.

24 LOWRY PUEBLO

Distance: 0.3 mile (0.4 km) plus exploring
Elevation gain: 25 feet (7.6 m)
High point: 6736 feet (2053 m)
Difficulty: Easy
Trail surface: Dirt
Map: Trails Illustrated Durango Cortez
GPS: 37.5846379°N, 108.9226902°W
Note: Leashed dogs allowed; pit toilets at trailhead; no water access

> Named after local homesteader George Lowry, Lowry Pueblo was designated a National Historic Landmark in 1967 and became part of Canyons of the Ancients National Monument in 2000. Lowry Pueblo is the only developed site within the monument with stabilized walls. The uppermost levels are currently in view; the lower levels remain preserved under the dirt. This short accessible interpretive loop trail and picnic area are open year-round, but winters bring deep snow.

GETTING THERE

From the town of Dolores, follow State Highway 145 west for about 3 miles (4.8 km) to CO 184 and turn right to head west. In 8 miles (13 km), reach US 491 at Lewis. Turn right

WHAT'S IN A NAME?

When archaeologists discover and document archaeological sites, they often name the site with a number. Sometimes these sites are named for the person that discovered them, for the location, or for the shape or design. Native Americans often give sites names that have meaning to their tribe or ancestors.

The Lowry Pueblo was once home to around one hundred people.

(north) onto US 491 and follow it for 9.4 miles (15 km). Turn left (west) onto County Road CC and follow it for 8.4 miles (13.5 km). Turn left onto CR 7.25 and follow signs 0.2 mile (0.3 km) to Lowry Pueblo parking area.

ON THE TRAIL

From the parking lot, head to the right on the trail to walk it counterclockwise. The trail is fairly flat as it meanders toward the pueblo. What about this area would make you consider building a village in this location? Imagine life back in the Ancestral Puebloan time. The inhabitants were said to be farmers that made pottery and cotton for trade. Be on the lookout for shards of pottery along the trail. Remember that if you find something, leave it for other visitors to discover on their visit.

Don't miss the interpretive signs along the trail to garner new information about this community. The Puebloans were also small-game hunters—along the trail you may see animals similar to what they hunted, from deer to rabbits. Many species call the area around the pueblo home: squirrels, lizards, and snakes. More than a hundred bird species can be

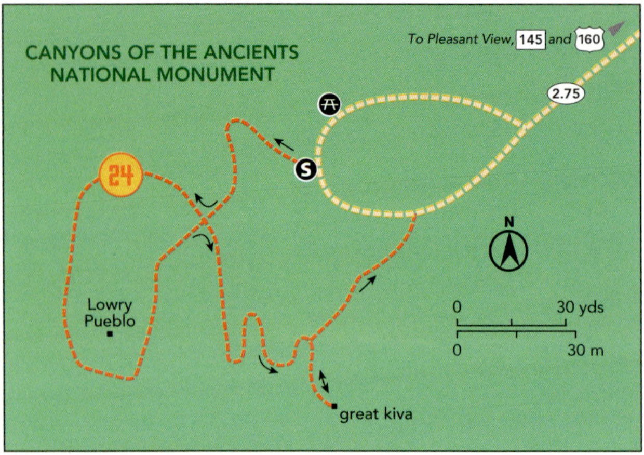

found within the monument. When the pueblo comes into view, you are at the high point on the trail.

At 0.1 mile (0.2 km), the pueblo is on the left-hand side. Part of the pueblo is under roof protection, while other sections are exposed to the elements. Once home to approximately a hundred people, this Chaco Canyon–style pueblo featured forty rooms and eight kivas.

Descend a short set of stairs to enter the pueblo area and explore. Visit the site respectfully. Remember that oils from your hands can transfer, so do not touch the walls. Close your eyes to take yourself back in time as you pass through the original doors and narrow passageways. You can spend a lot of time here noticing the difference in the rooms, including the thickness of the walls. Notice the wood from the juniper trees, used to stabilize the homes and create the rooftops for the village rooms. Does the village look similar to the pueblos in Mesa Verde National Park or Hawkins Preserve (Hike 19)?

Continue on the trail counterclockwise to the eastern edge of the village and the great kiva, 0.1 mile (0.2 km) from the pueblo, 0.2 mile (0.3 km) from the start. The great kiva

The great kiva is nearly 50 feet in diameter.

is almost 50 feet (15 m) in diameter. Feel free to explore the kiva as well. With the exposure to the elements, it is not preserved as well as the pueblo. The stones in the floor of the great kiva have been interpreted by today's Hopi Indians to represent winter and summer people. Do you see the winter and summer people on the floor?

Kivas were said to be used for large gatherings. While you can't use this one to gather, after exploring the ceremonial site, continue on the loop trail to the trailhead in about 0.1 mile (0.2 km) from the great kiva. Here you can enjoy a meal or snack at the picnic area near the trailhead. Be prepared for a visit from chipmunks if you have some food here.

25 PAINTED HAND PUEBLO

Distance: 0.8 mile (1.3 km)
Elevation gain: 150 feet (45 m)
High point: 6079 feet (1852 m)
Difficulty: Easy
Trail surface: Dirt, slickrock, sand
Map: Trails Illustrated Durango Cortez

The Painted Hand Pueblo was part of a small village with twenty rooms.

GPS: 37.45396°N, 108.97202°W
Note: Leashed dogs allowed; seasonal pit toilets at trailhead; no water access

> The Painted Hand Pueblo, recognized on the National Register of Historic Places, features a small village of about twenty rooms constructed around CE 1200 and a petroglyph featuring hands—hence its name. The rocky, rutted road requires a high-clearance vehicle. After recent rain, it may be impassible, but you can park on the shoulder and walk 1 mile (1.6 km) to the trailhead. There is no shade on this hike, so bring water and a hat.

GETTING THERE

From the town of Dolores, follow State Highway 145 west for about 3 miles (4.8 km) to CO 184 and turn right to head west. In 8 miles (13 km), reach US 491 at Lewis. Turn right (north) onto US 491 and follow it for about 7 miles (11 km) to County Road BB—look for a sign for Hovenweep National Monument. Measure your mileage from this turnoff. Turn left (west) onto CR BB and follow it about 5.7 miles (9.1 km) to CR 10. Turn left (south) onto CR 10 and continue following the Hovenweep signs. In about 11.7 miles (19 km), turn left onto CR 4531—look for a kiosk with a map. A high-clearance vehicle is recommended because of a few rocky sections of road. In 1 mile (1.6 km), turn left into the small, rocky parking area and trailhead.

ON THE TRAIL

The Painted Hand Pueblo trail leads from the parking lot across the canyon rim. Almost immediately, you can see the beauty of the area. On a clear day, you may be able to see Sleeping Ute Mountain, about 15 miles (24 km) away. It doesn't take long before you have a view from the trail of some of the towers in the distance.

After about 0.2 mile (0.3 km), stay left to follow the sign and descend between two large rocks. In 0.3 mile (0.4 km),

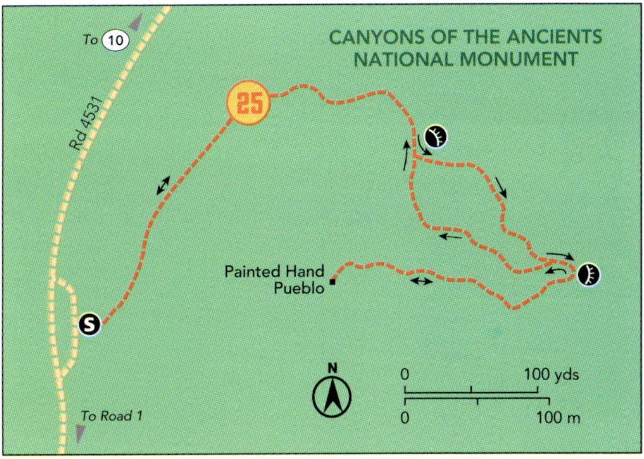

Painted hands can be seen below the Painted Hand Pueblo.

reach a junction with the other end of a short loop trail. Continue straight and shortly reach a viewpoint looking down at the site.

The trail makes a sharp bend and at 0.4 mile (0.6 km) descends to Painted Hand Pueblo. Underneath the pueblo, there are very faint pictographs of handprints—look at them but do not touch them. Oils and other things transferred from hands (along with weathering) have caused the pictographs to become fainter and fainter over time. You can also see soot from fires used for cooking.

Remember that Canyons of the Ancients did not become a national monument until 2000. Therefore, preservation of its sites has been limited. Use caution when exploring around the fragile towers on this hike. Explore and observe at your own pace. Reflect and marvel at the design and craftsmanship of the pueblo and towers. The cryptobiotic soil around the trail is also fragile, so it is important to stay on the path.

As you view the towers, look for shards of pottery. You may pick up and look at the pottery, but remember to leave the pieces you found around the site. Painted milkvetch and other wildflowers line the trail, and collared lizards are common. You might spot a Mesa Verde night snake out looking for a meal. Solitude and quiet are one of the draws of this hike.

To return to the trailhead, retrace your steps to just past the viewpoint and stay left to take the slightly longer but gentler—yet still rocky—leg of this loop. Rock gabions and wooden signs help guide you no matter what route you take. Either way, the entire route is still less than 1 mile (1.6 km). As you cross the canyon top, listen to the birdsong. Look across the canyon one last time before you leave this remote site.

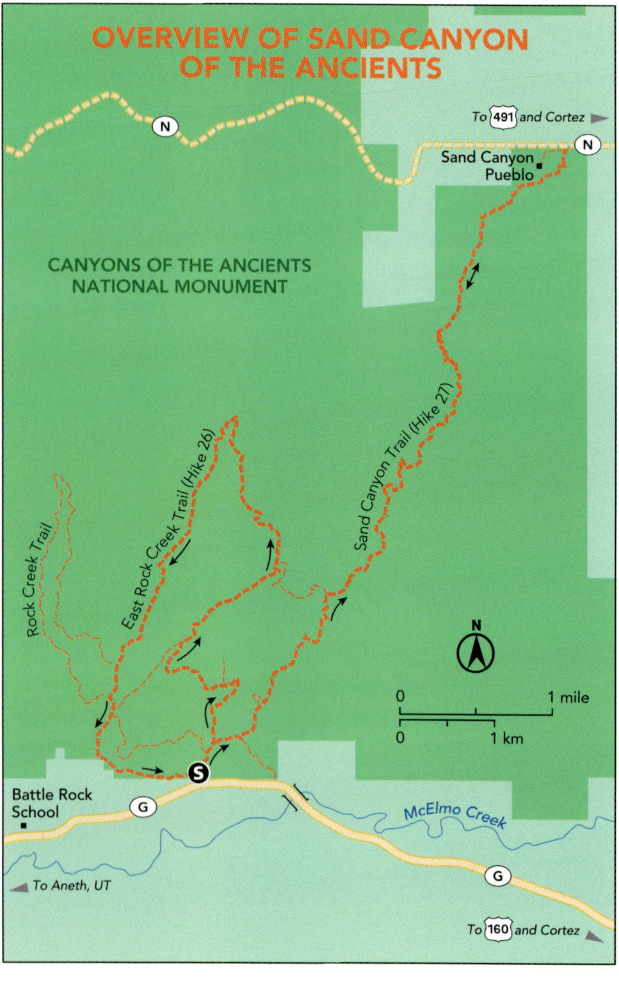
OVERVIEW OF SAND CANYON OF THE ANCIENTS
To 491 and Cortez
N
Sand Canyon Pueblo
CANYONS OF THE ANCIENTS NATIONAL MONUMENT
Sand Canyon Trail (Hike 27)
East Rock Creek Trail (Hike 26)
Rock Creek Trail
N
0
1 mile
0
1 km
S
Battle Rock School
G
McElmo Creek
To Aneth, UT
G
To 160 and Cortez

SAND CANYON AND ROCK CREEK

Canyon of the Ancients National Monument covers a vast swath of Southwestern Colorado along the border with Utah. The national monument boasts the United States' highest concentration of archaeological sites, with over 8500 recorded since 2022 and an estimated 30,000 sites said to still be undocumented or undiscovered. From the Colorado side, access roads reach into the canyons from US 491 between the towns of Dove Creek on the north and Cortez on the south.

The Sand Canyon and Rock Creek area encompasses a large number of acres in the monument west of Cortez. The Sand Canyon area—restricted to trail access only for hikers, horseback riders, and bicyclists (bicyclists yield to hikers and horses, hikers yield to horses)—is accessed from US 160 just south of Cortez on County Road G, which follows McElmo Creek west toward Aneth, Utah. Near the Sand Canyon trailhead is Castle Rock Pueblo, and the Sand Canyon Trail leads to Sand Canyon Pueblo, as well as other sites along the way. Water isn't available in this remote area, so bring plenty.

26 EAST ROCK CREEK LOOP

Distance: 7.2 miles (11 km)
Elevation gain: 705 feet (214 m)

Sand Canyon's sandstone walls contain many intriguing geological features.

High point: 5850 feet (1783 m)
Difficulty: Moderate
Trail surface: Dirt, slickrock, roots, rocks
Map: Trails Illustrated Durango Cortez
GPS: 37.3415444°N, 110.9270833°W
Note: Leashed dogs allowed; portable toilet at trailhead; no water access

> Within Sand Canyon, the East Rock Creek loop, shared with horses and mountain bikers, showcases the monument. Life for the Ancestral Puebloans can be seen along this trail and across the canyon: many archaeological sites are not named or documented on maps. There is little to no shade so bring water and a hat. Areas of wash may have water depending on recent weather. The best time for this hike is spring and September through October.

GETTING THERE

From the town of Cortez, drive south on US 491/160 for 3.4 miles (5.5 km) to McElmo Canyon Road (County

Road G)—look for the sign for Hovenweep National Monument. Turn right (west) onto CR G and drive for 12 miles (19 km). Soon after you cross a bridge, the trailhead is on the right. Park at the second trailhead for Sand Canyon South.

ON THE TRAIL

From the parking lot, follow the slickrock trail straight. At 0.1 mile (0.2 km), the Castle Rock Pueblo is on your right. Take a side trail to check out this site built in the late Pueblo III period. Approximately 75 to 150 people lived here from CE 1260s until 1280 when the Puebloans fled due to an attack. With limited excavation, sixteen kivas were discovered by Crow Canyon Archaeological Center archaeologists, along with nine possible towers, forty aboveground rooms, and a D-shaped enclosure.

Shortly after the pueblo, the trail reaches a junction with a connector trail; continue straight ahead to follow the orange diamond signs telling you to continue up the slickrock. Wildflowers, cactus, and piñon pines line the sides of the slickrock, sometimes growing between the cracks. The monsoons of spring and summer bring out the barrel cactus blossoms and pods on the yucca trees.

At a sign at 0.3 mile (0.5 km), reach a junction with the blue diamond connector trail on the right to the Sand Canyon Trail; stay left on the lower connector trail. At 0.6 mile (1 km), you can see one of a few unnamed archaeological sites across the canyon walls. Continue along the connector trail, which winds around as it contours the canyon. In about 0.25 mile (0.4 km), a spur trail on the right at about 0.9 mile (1.4 km) heads up to get a closer look at the dwelling.

The hoodoo rocks at 1 mile (1.6 km) may remind you of faces. Another dwelling comes into view at 1.1 miles (1.7 km) up on the sandstone cliffs. This is the perfect spot to test your echo as you take in the views of the dwelling. Red-tailed hawks, crows, and bluebirds soar over the sandstone.

The trail continues, with a spire on the right at just shy of 1.5 miles (2.4 km). Lizards dart around rocks and brush, trying to find bits of shade. On hot days, remember to take frequent water breaks, and consider sucking on bits of Mormon tea while hiking to keep your mouth moist.

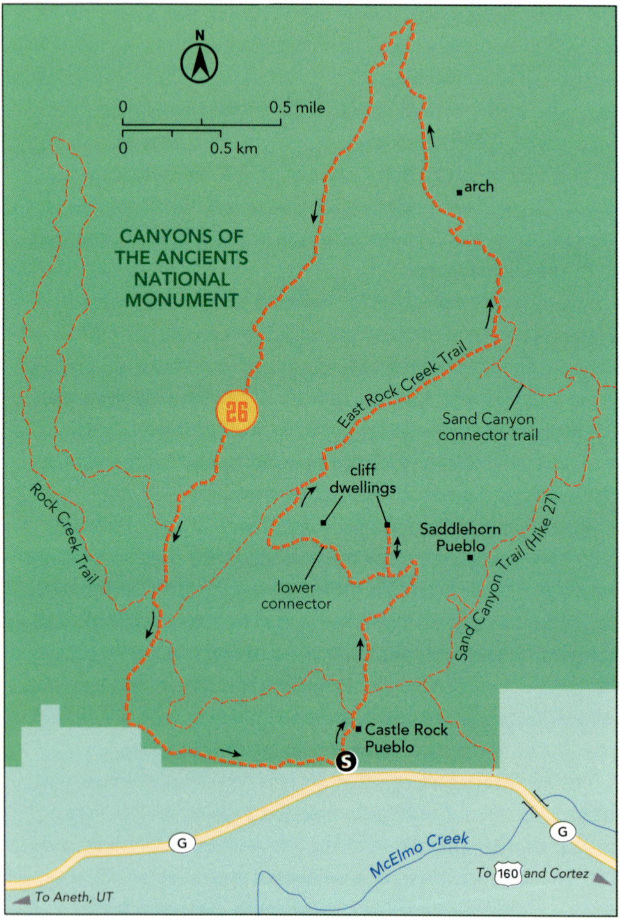

There is an unnamed cliff dwelling along the East Rock Creek Trail.

At a junction at around 1.6 miles (2.5 km) with a trail to the left, continue straight to follow the green diamond trail signs for the East Rock Creek Trail. Heading counterclockwise on this loop, you begin to climb. Shortly after, a "Stay on Designated Trail" sign reminds you of Leave No Trace principles. Rattlesnakes are found in Sand Canyon, and the cryptobiotic soil crust in the canyon is fragile.

At 2.6 miles (4.1 km), the Sand Canyon connector trail is on the right; stay left to continue on the East Rock Creek Trail down into the wash. Rodents, rabbits, and foxes frequent the canyon.

At 3.1 miles (4.9 km), you come upon the East Rock Creek Canyon arch, which resembles a rainbow. You may spot elk, deer, or coyotes if you hike near dawn or dusk. An uphill stretch at 3.8 miles (6.1 km) heads the trail back south toward the trailhead. It leads into areas of wash that may have water in them after a storm.

A large section of wash occurs at around 4.3 miles (6.9 km). Look left for good views of the arch now. Bears, marmots, and mountain lions may also be seen in the canyon. The trail becomes more rocky and rugged at 5 miles (8 km).

At 5.5 miles (8.8 km), avoid the wash off-trail. A large rock at 5.7 miles (9.1 km) shows geological periods of time. At around 5.8 miles (9.3 km), the trail meets the Rock Creek Trail on the right; continue straight on the East Rock Creek Trail. At 6 miles (9.6 km), the yellow diamonds of the other end of the Rock Creek Trail come into view on the right; continue straight.

At 6.2 miles (9.9 km), reach a trail junction. Straight ahead is the middle connector trail; to the left is the other end of the East Rock Creek Trail. Stay to the right on the upper connector trail that heads down the wash. At 6.5 miles (10 km), you may hear water and will see the monument boundary fencing. Homes and a museum of some old cars appear on the right. A metal marker on the right notes that this area was part of a cadastral survey in 2002.

Continue to follow the trail east along the fence line. Farm animals, including chickens, may greet you along the fence with their songs. A Department of Interior sign on the left-hand side is at just shy of 7 miles (11 km). The trail continues east to the slickrock that began the hike. At the trail junction near CR G, turn left to head down the slickrock back to the second trailhead.

27 SAND CANYON

Distance: 12 miles (19.3 km), plus exploring
Elevation gain: 1960 feet (597 m)
High point: 6863 feet (2091 m)
Difficulty: Challenging
Trail surface: Dirt, slickrock, roots, rocks
Map: Trails Illustrated Durango Cortez
GPS: 37.3415444°N, 110.9270833°W
Note: Leashed dogs allowed; portable toilet at trailhead; no water access

Sand Canyon offers views in all directions.

Sand Canyon encompasses many acres in Canyons of the Ancients National Monument. The Sand Canyon Trail, shared with horses and mountain bikers, is the most popular trail in the canyon due to its many archaeological sites. There is little to no shade, so bring water and a hat. Areas of wash may have water, depending on recent weather. The best time to enjoy this hike is spring and September through October.

GETTING THERE

From the town of Cortez, drive south on US 491/160 for 3.4 miles (5.4 km) to McElmo Canyon Road (County Road G)—look for the sign for Hovenweep National Monument. Turn right (west) onto CR G and drive west for 12 miles (19 km). Soon after you cross a bridge, the Sand Canyon South trailhead is on the right near Battle Rock. Park at the second trailhead.

To start at the Sand Canyon North trailhead (or to leave a shuttle there), from Cortez drive north on US 491 for 5.3 miles (8.5 km) to CR P on the left. Turn left (west) onto CR P and follow it 4.4 miles (7 km). Turn left (south) onto CR 18

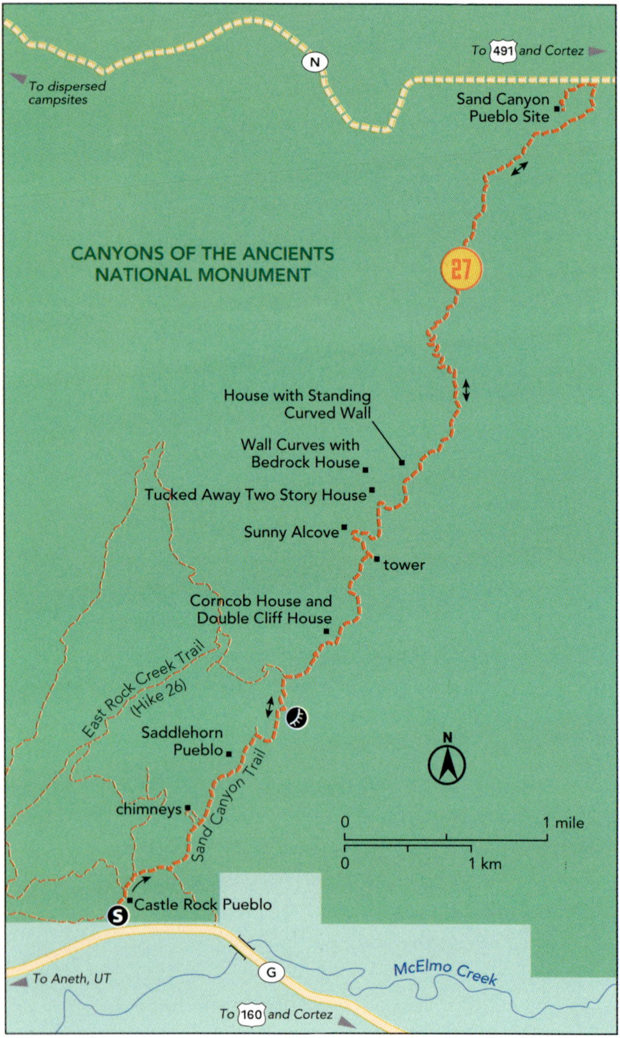
To 491 and Cortez
N
To dispersed campsites
Sand Canyon Pueblo Site
CANYONS OF THE ANCIENTS NATIONAL MONUMENT
27
House with Standing Curved Wall
Wall Curves with Bedrock House
Tucked Away Two Story House
Sunny Alcove
tower
Corncob House and Double Cliff House
East Rock Creek Trail (Hike 26)
Saddlehorn Pueblo
Sand Canyon Trail
N
chimneys
0
1 mile
0
1 km
Castle Rock Pueblo
S
To Aneth, UT
G
McElmo Creek
To 160 and Cortez

and drive 0.5 mile (0.8 km) to CR P, then turn right (west) onto CR P. Follow it for 2.5 miles (4 km). Turn left onto CR 16 for 0.9 mile (1.4 km). Turn right on CR N to reach the trailhead in 1 mile (1.6 km).

ON THE TRAIL

There are several ways to enjoy this hike. If the full 12 miles (19 km) is too much, leave a car at either the south or north trailhead and drive to the other trailhead to start a one-way hike of 6 miles (9.6 km). Starting at the Sand Canyon North trailhead requires descending 0.5 mile (0.8 km) of switchbacks; starting at the Sand Canyon South trailhead requires climbing the switchbacks' elevation gain of 700 feet (213 m). You can also walk in from either trailhead for as many miles as you want and turn around to return to where you started. Starting at the south trailhead is much easier and you can see plenty of sites, including Saddlehorn Pueblo, Corncob House, and Sunny Alcove House, before the switchbacks, skipping that section altogether if you wish.

This out-and-back hike of the full trail starts at the Sand Canyon South trailhead. From the parking lot, follow the slickrock trail straight. At 0.1 mile (0.2 km), the Castle Rock Pueblo is on your right. Take a side trail to check out this site built in the late Pueblo III period. Approximately 75 to 150 people lived here from CE 1260s until 1280 when the Ancestral Puebloans fled due to an attack. With limited excavation, sixteen kivas were discovered by Crow Canyon Archaeological Center archaeologists, along with nine possible towers, forty aboveground rooms, and a D-shaped enclosure.

Shortly after the pueblo, the trail reaches a junction with a connector trail; continue straight ahead to follow the orange diamond signs telling you to continue up the slickrock. Wildflowers, cactus, and piñon pines line the sides of the slickrock, sometimes growing between the cracks.

The walls of one intact room can be found at Tucked Away Two Story House.

At a sign at 0.3 mile (0.5 km), reach a junction with the blue diamond connector trail to the left to the East Rock Creek Trail (Hike 26). Continue straight, following the yellow diamonds, to stay on the Sand Canyon Trail. At 0.5 mile (0.8 km), reach another trail junction to the right; continue straight to stay on the Sand Canyon Trail. Signs, maps, and cairns keep you on the right track through the canyon.

As you make your way to the Saddlehorn Pueblo, several spur trails off to the left take you to unnamed archaeological sites, including one at 0.7 mile (1.1 km) where the sites look like several chimneys. From here, the trail begins to narrow and meander up and down.

At about 1 mile (1.6 km), the Saddlehorn Pueblo comes into view on the left-hand side. Built into the alcove, this dwelling has two rooms protected by the canyon walls. Two structures are about 100 feet (30 m) above the alcove on a pinnacle. It is suggested that there were sleeping rooms and cooking rooms with pottery found. Occupied from approximately CE 1250 until about 1285, the pinnacles could have been used for defense or communication. A kiva discovered in the late 1980s was backfilled for preservation purposes. BLM refers to the pueblo as the Saddlehorn Hamlet.

Don't miss the spur on the right at around 1.5 miles (2.4 km), which takes you to a beautiful canyon view. Shy of 2 miles (3.2 km)—1.7 miles (2.7 km) without exploring all the spur trails—you reach the second connector trail on the left-hand side that leads to the East Rock Creek Trail (Hike 26); continue straight ahead on the Sand Canyon Trail. Remember, these mileages depend on how much exploring you do and how many spur trails you take.

The trail banks to the right and narrows. About 0.25 mile (0.4 km) past the connector trail—2.25 miles (3.6 km) from the start—the trail descends multiple switchbacks. A cairn on the right lets you know you are on the right track. At 2.3 miles (3.7 km), a mini slot on the left is a cool spot to take a break, eat some snacks, and let young hikers climb a rock. A spur trail on the left takes you to two sites: Corncob House and Double Cliff House.

FLASH FLOODS

Flash floods are the number one cause of weather-related deaths in the United States. Flash flooding is common in Canyons of the Ancients National Park, especially in Sand Canyon. Know the flood risk for the area you are visiting before heading out to hike: monitor the National Oceanic and Atmospheric Administration (NOAA) weather radio bulletin or other reliable source. Checking conditions at a visitor center is always smart.

While hiking, stay alert for potential rain and rising water levels. If flooding occurs, get to higher ground immediately. If you encounter an area already flooded, avoid it. Do not attempt to cross any water, especially if it is flowing fast. Remember the slogan "Turn around—don't drown."

A horned lizard finds shade on the wide open trail.

Built on two ledges in an alcove, Double Cliff House is well preserved from the overhang. A ladder was used to access the upper rooms, one of which has a window. The first record of the site was in 1965. Pottery found onsite suggests occupation around CE 1200.

To the west of Double Cliff is Corncob House. With only one alcove, the home site is much smaller, and erosion has occurred. Also excavated in 1965, the home got its name from the ancient corncobs found during documentation. Along these spur trails, you can find good places to test your echo against the canyon walls.

The trail gets easier as it continues up the canyon. In another 0.25 mile (0.4 km)—2.5 miles (4 km) from the start—take the spur trail on the right to the site of a tower. More than likely, it was used for communication throughout the inhabited areas of Sand Canyon. In about 0.2 mile (0.3 km) from the tower, a trail on the left leads to Sunny Alcove, which featured eight rooms and a kiva. When researching this area in 1965, archaeologists came upon many artifacts, including manos and metates, pottery, and corncobs. The inhabitants of Sunny Alcove built shelves in the walls and even had wooden latches in the doorways.

As you continue up the canyon, red-tailed hawks, crows, and bluebirds soar over the sandstone. Have you seen any collared or horned lizards? Sometimes they are evident in such abundance that you lose count of how many you have seen. Also not to be missed is the prickly pear cactus or the white-stemmed evening primrose.

At about 3.3 miles (5.3 km), take the short side canyon on the left to Tucked Away Two Story House. Notice how this dwelling really matches the shape of the alcove, giving it its name. Walls curved at the back and squared off at the front offered protection and obscurity.

Adjacent to Tucked Away Two Story house is what remains of Wall Curves with Bedrock House off to the left in another alcove. Notice the second-story doorway and a window in the south wall. Pottery found by archaeologists date the occupation to CE 1100–1300.

At about 3.7 miles (6 km), the seventh and last named site before the Sand Canyon Pueblo is the House with Standing Curved Wall. A 38-foot-long (11.5 m) curved wall, featuring a window, still stands today. Very few artifacts were found at this dwelling, the highest-elevation cliff dwelling on this trail. Have a snack and drink some water at around 4 miles (6.4 km) to prepare for the switchbacks just up the trail.

At 4.5 miles (7.2 km)—your GPS may be closer to 5 miles (8 km) depending on the additional mileage you hiked on the spur trails—you come to the hardest part of the trail: a steep and rocky 0.5 mile (0.8 km) that contains thirty switchbacks. A wooden sign denotes the start of this difficult section. Take your time as the elevation gains 700 feet (213 m) in a very short time. Many hikers turn around at this point to do a shorter out and back. For this hike, continue up the switchbacks.

After the switchbacks, the trail is much like the early sections, with small rises and red sand. Enjoy the canyon views of the Navajo and Entrada Sandstones. Sandy benches comprise the Carmel Formation. If you look closely at the limestone, can you find any evidence of marine fossils?

At 6 miles (9.6 km), you come to the end of the trail. Off to the left of the north trailhead sits the largest site in the Four Corners region: the Sand Canyon Pueblo, built around CE 1250. Looting, erosion, and other factors have contributed to the destruction of the pueblo over time. Excavated in the 1980s and '90s, it has been backfilled for preservation. Only trees and the foundational walls can be seen today. A U-shaped wall surrounds hundreds of rooms, a plaza, kivas, and a great kiva.

Informational signs explain about the areas that have been backfilled, so visitors can imagine the village that was said to be home to up to six hundred Ancestral Puebloans. Multiple towers outside the wall served as lookouts for spotting enemies heading toward the village. A drought in CE 1276 saw the migration of some inhabitants. Historians believe an attack around CE 1277 took the lives of many of those who lived in the village. The survivors fled toward New Mexico and Arizona.

If you do the hike as a shuttle, this is the point where your hike through Sand Canyon ends. For this roundtrip hike, have some snacks and head back on the trail to the south trailhead. Take your time on the switchbacks section, as descending the 700 feet (213 m) can be just as challenging as ascending it.

If you skipped any of the spur trails, on the way back take time to see where the paths lead. Even if you saw all seven sites, you may want to explore them again to see if you discover anything new with a second look. Back at the trailhead, you may feel a sense of wonder and awe at this little peek into the life of the Ancestral Puebloans that builds an appreciation of their ingenuity and the hardships they faced.

OPPOSITE: *Hovenweep Castle is the main attraction of the Square Tower Loop (Hike 28).*

PART 4: HOVENWEEP NATIONAL MONUMENT

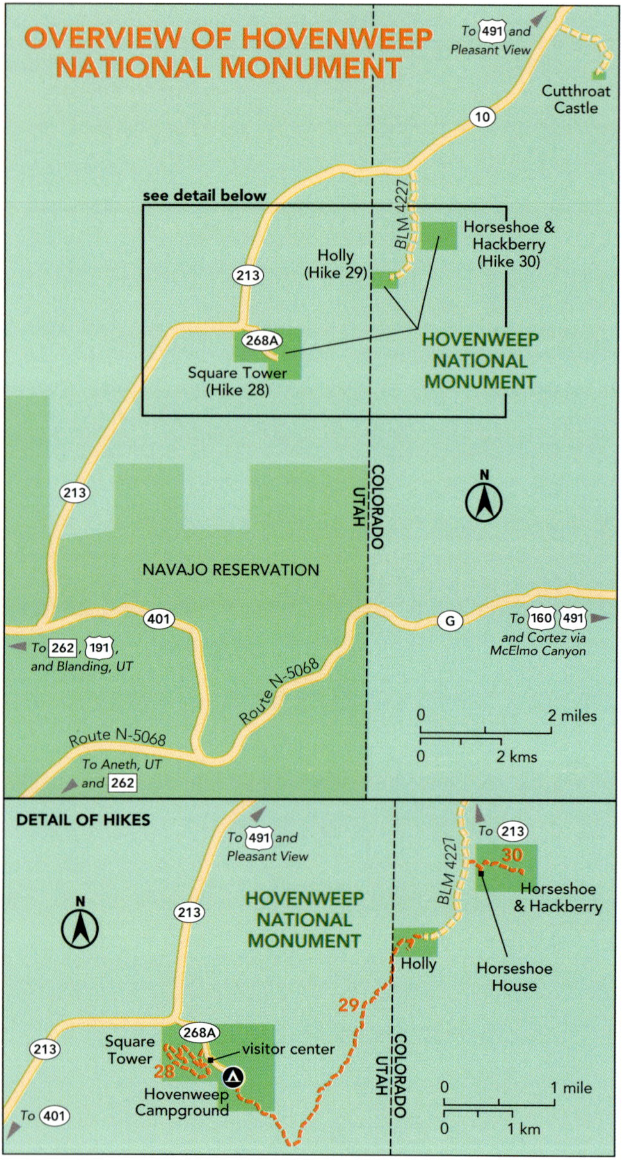

OVERVIEW OF HOVENWEEP NATIONAL MONUMENT
To 491 and Pleasant View
Cutthroat Castle
10
see detail below
BLM 4227
Horseshoe & Hackberry (Hike 30)
Holly (Hike 29)
213
268A
Square Tower (Hike 28)
HOVENWEEP NATIONAL MONUMENT
COLORADO
UTAH
N
NAVAJO RESERVATION
401
G
To 262, 191, and Blanding, UT
To 160 491 and Cortez via McElmo Canyon
Route N-5068
To Aneth, UT and 262
0 2 miles
0 2 kms
DETAIL OF HIKES
To 491 and Pleasant View
To 213
30
Horseshoe & Hackberry
Holly
Horseshoe House
29
Square Tower
visitor center
28
Hovenweep Campground
To 401
0 1 mile
0 1 km

VISITOR CENTER AREA

Derived from the Ute word for "deserted valley," Hovenweep was established as a 784-acre (317 hectare) national monument in 1923. Hovenweep was occupied by Ancestral Puebloans as far back as two thousand years ago, with multistory stone dwellings built from CE 1200 to 1300. The remnants of six villages—pueblos, cliff dwellings, and towers—stretch from southeastern Utah just north of the Navajo Reservation into Southwestern Colorado.

The three hikes in this book are on the Utah side of the monument. Thunderstorms and lightning are common in the area. Late spring and summer bring biting gnats (no-see-ums) to this side of the monument. Hovenweep is a remote area accessed by paved county roads and unpaved roads that can be hard to get to in rainy or snowy weather. At the visitor center, staffed year-round, there is a campground, but the nearest services are 14 miles (22.5 km) southeast at Ismay Trading Post on County Road G.

28 SQUARE TOWER LOOP

Distance: 2 miles (3.2 km)
Elevation gain: 220 feet (67 m)
High point: 5249 feet (1599 m)
Difficulty: Easy
Trail surface: Pavement, dirt, slickrock, canyon wash
Maps: Trails Illustrated Utah, Trails Illustrated Colorado

This is one of the many square towers in Little Ruin Canyon.

GPS: 38.6026965°N, 110.038966°W

Note: Leashed dogs allowed; restrooms and water access at visitor center

> Sometimes referred to as "Hovenweep's Home Base" because of its proximity to the monument's visitor center, the Square Tower Loop takes you within viewing distance of some of Hovenweep's most impressive towers, houses, and even the Hovenweep Castle. Because of the structures' fragility, visitors may view them only from a distance. This exposed trail features little to no shade. Pick up a brochure at the visitor center for a self-guided look at the Ancestral Puebloans.

GETTING THERE

From Pleasant View on US 491, turn left (west) onto County Road CC and follow it 5 miles (8 km). Turn left (south) onto

CR 10 and follow it 22 miles (35 km); it becomes CR 213 over the state line in Utah. Turn left onto Hovenweep Access Road (CR 268A) and park on the right at the visitor center.

From Cortez, take US 491/160 south for 2 miles (3.2 km). Turn right (west) onto McElmo Canyon Road (CR G) and follow it 30 miles (48 km), into Utah. Turn right onto Cajon Mesa Road (CR 401, or Route 2416) and follow it 4 miles (6.4 km). Turn right onto CR 213 (N-5069, or Route 2422) and follow it 6 miles (9.6 km). Turn right onto Hovenweep Access Road (CR 268A) and park on the right at the visitor center.

ON THE TRAIL

The Square Tower Loop trail begins at the visitor center on a paved walk to an overlook of Little Ruin Canyon in a shy 0.2 mile (0.3 km). From here, you may go left (clockwise) or right (counterclockwise) around the loop. This hike heads left (clockwise). Interpretive signs detail the different vegetation in the canyon, from sagebrush and Mormon tea to

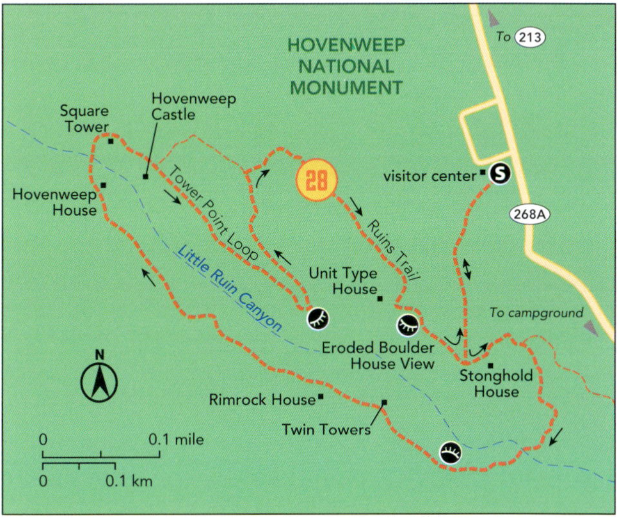

Hovenweep Castle can be seen from a distance.

Utah juniper and cliffrose, and name the structures you see along the hike.

At a little less than 0.3 mile (0.5 km), you reach the cutoff trail on the left for the campground; stay right on the Ruins Trail. At 0.25 mile (0.4 km), a bench provides a quiet place for reflection. The hike becomes more rugged and begins descending into the canyon. On the canyon floor, you cross a creek bed. Do you see any birds of prey flying above the canyon?

The trail begins to climb at a little over 0.3 mile (0.5 km) toward the canyon rim. Look across the canyon for views on the right. The trail switchbacks up a mix of rock steps and artificial steps. At about 0.4 mile (0.6 km), you get your first look at Twin Towers from a distance.

At the top of the canyon rim, you can see the Twin Towers up close and personal. Ten buildings are visible from the canyon rim, while several others can be seen below the rim. Over thirty kivas have been found in the Square Tower Group, suggesting that a few thousand people once lived here.

At a little over 0.5 mile (0.8 km), Rimrock House can be seen as you continue along the rim. Take some time to see each structure from every viewpoint and angle. From the rim, be sure to also look down for any hidden structures.

As you make your way, at around 0.8 mile (1.3 km) look down into the canyon on the right to see Square Tower. Look straight across the canyon to see the back of Hovenweep Castle. To the left of the castle is Hovenweep House. As the trail begins to sweep around the edge of the canyon walls, Hovenweep House is now an up-close view. It is a structure where you can get a bit of a view of the inside.

A bench on the right-hand side at just shy of 1 mile (1.6 km) is perfect for getting an overlook of the Square Tower group. Drink some water before continuing. Some shade can be found before you see evidence of a check dam. At a trail junction where a sign directs you left to head to the visitor center on the Ruins Trail, continue straight ahead onto the Tower Point Loop. Nearby is Hovenweep Castle—be sure to read the sign and look at the 1935 photos of the castle's restoration.

At about 1.2 miles (1.9 km) reach a viewpoint of Little Ruin Canyon. Here the trail takes a sharp bend to follow the canyon rim. At a little over 1.4 miles (2.2 km), the other end of the Tower Point Loop hits another junction with the Ruins Trail. Turn right to follow the Ruins Trail back toward the visitor center.

You can view Unit Type House at 1.6 miles (2.5 km). Across the canyon is what remains of Eroded Boulder House. Friendly ravens singing songs and taking a break along the dwelling walls are common in this area.

At 1.8 miles (2.9 km) Stronghold House is the last structure you view from this trail. Shortly you reach the paved path on the left and follow it to head back to the visitor center.

29 HOLLY GROUP

Distance: 7 miles (11 km)
Elevation gain: 646 feet (196 m)
High point: 8200 feet (2499 m)
Difficulty: Moderate
Trail surface: Dirt, slickrock, canyon wash
Maps: Trails Illustrated Utah, Trails Illustrated Colorado
GPS: 38.6026965°N, 110.038966°W
Note: Leashed dogs allowed; restroom and water access at campground

> Holly site is named after local rancher James Holly, who hosted archaeologists in Hovenweep in the early 1900s. This out-and-back hike passes through two short slot canyons, 18 inches (45 cm) wide and 35–58 feet (10.6–17 m) long. A day pack is fine through the slots, but a backpack might not fit. Check weather, as rain may fill the slots with water. There is no shade, so get an early start in summer.

GETTING THERE

From Pleasant View on US 491, turn left (west) onto County Road CC and follow it 5 miles (8 km). Turn left (south) on CR 10 and follow it 22 miles (35 km); it becomes CR 213 over the state line in Utah. Turn left onto Hovenweep Access Road (CR 268A) into the monument and follow it to the visitor center. Continue 0.25 mile (0.4 km) past the visitor center to the campground and day-use parking lot.

From Cortez, take US 491/160 south for 2 miles (3.2 km). Turn right (west) onto McElmo Canyon Road (CR G) and follow it through McElmo Canyon for 30 miles (48 km), into Utah. Turn right onto Cajon Mesa Road (CR 401, or Route 2416) and follow it 4 miles (6.4 km). Turn right onto CR 213 (N-5069, or Route 2422) and continue for 6 miles (9.6 km). Turn right onto Hovenweep Access Road (CR 268A) into the

Several towers still stand at the Holly site.

monument and follow it to the visitor center. Continue 0.25 mile (0.4 km) past the visitor center to the campground and day-use parking lot.

ON THE TRAIL

You can start this trail either at the visitor center campground or from County Road 10 near the Holly site. This hike begins from the campground, where wooden signs and rocks guide you to the trailhead. Be sure to sign the trail registry before heading out.

The trail descends southeast across slickrock. Follow the cairns. At about 0.1 mile (0.2 km), you will be hiking through the first mini slot. After climbing through the slot, you can see views of Keeley Canyon. In about 160 feet (48 m), you encounter rock stairs, and in another 160 feet (48 m) the trail takes you into the wash. Sagebrush and piñon pine line the trail.

At 0.25 mile (0.4 km), a brown trail sign says to continue left. Cactus, Mormon tea, and Indian paintbrush bloom along the trail from April to August. Ravens, hawks, and golden eagles are often spotted soaring above the monument.

At almost 0.5 mile (0.8 km), there is a section of barbed-wire fencing. At this point, you leave the visitor center section of the monument and enter Bureau of Land Management territory. Follow the sign into the wash again. Continue to follow the cairns.

At just shy of 1 mile (1.6 km), a BLM sign indicates the trail heads to the left, now heading northeast. An additional brown sign guides you out of the wash. The trail continues up and down and across the wash. Watch out for cows and cow pies as the trail continues to meander in and out of the wash. At 1.5 miles (2.4 km), a rock on the right may remind you of an elephant or perhaps an AT-AT Walker from Star

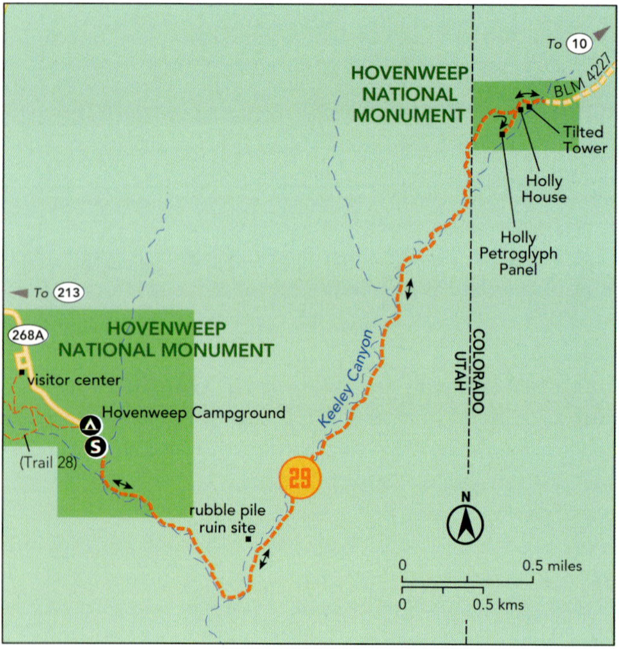

The slot canyons add some mystery and fun to the trail.

Wars. Great rocks lining the trail provide a perfect place to sit to drink some water and have a snack. Be sure to watch your feet as you sit on the rocks: there are ten species of snakes in the monument, including rattlesnakes.

When you reach 2.4 miles (3.8 km), another wash joins in from the left (north). A sign indicates what remains of a dwelling you can see on the left-hand side of the trail. Climbing a hill at 2.9 miles (4.6 km) wakes up your legs before you encounter the second slot canyon.

You go through a barbed-wire fence again at a little over 3.3 miles (5.3 km) and leave BLM land to return to monument land. Shortly after, a wooden sign says to head left for a view of Holly Petroglyph Panel from an overlook. Head to the right for a closer view of the Holly Petroglyph Panel, hidden under a ledge. Archaeologists believe the panel represents the summer solstice, with spirals and a symbol of the sun. While it's hard to decipher, you can see some spirals and lines. After viewing the panel, backtrack and turn right, toward the Holly site, to see Holly House and Tilted Tower.

Reach the Holly site with multiple towers, including the two-story Holly Tower, Tilted Tower, and Holly House at about 3.5 miles (5.6 km). The Holly site seems in many ways to have been built for defense, as the structures were placed atop boulders, perhaps protecting the nearby seep.

After visiting the Holly site, follow the arrows at the junction to return the way you came, back toward the campground. Enjoy the slot canyons again and a view of Keeley Canyon from the opposite direction. Be sure to sign out at the trail registry when you reach the trailhead and campground.

30 HORSESHOE AND HACKBERRY

Distance: 1.4 miles (2.2 km)
Elevation gain: 91 feet (27 m)
High point: 5525 feet (1684 m)
Difficulty: Easy
Trail surface: Dirt, rock
Map: Trails Illustrated Mesa Verde

Hackberry was a large village, although most of the structures have collapsed.

GPS: 37.1973591°N, 108.4852942°W
Note: Dogs prohibited; pit toilet at midpoint of trail; no water access

> This out-and-back hike takes you through Hackberry Canyon to the Horseshoe and Hackberry groups. You can get a close view of the groups from afar; for safety and restoration purposes, the sites are roped off or not accessible. The trail on unimproved dirt roads is well marked with signs and cairns. You need a high-clearance vehicle to reach the trailhead, but that also means you may be the only visitor on the trail.

GETTING THERE

From Pleasant View on US 491, turn left (west) onto County Road CC and follow it 5 miles (8 km). Turn left (south) onto CR 10 and follow it 16 miles (25 km). Turn left (south) onto BLM 4227 and continue 1 mile (1.6 km) to the trailhead on the left.

From Cortez, take US 491/160 for 2 miles (3.2 km). Turn left onto McElmo Canyon Road (CR G) and follow it through McElmo Canyon for 30 miles (48 km), into Utah. Turn right onto Cajon Mesa Road (CR 401) and follow it 4 miles (6.4 km). Turn right onto CR 213 and continue east, past the visitor center road and back into Colorado, where it becomes CR 10. In 10 miles (16 km) from Cajon Mesa Road (CR 401), turn right onto BLM 4227 and continue 1 mile (1.6 km) to the trailhead on the left.

ON THE TRAIL

This hike starts by going downhill. From the beginning of the trail, you can spy Horseshoe Tower and Sleeping Ute Mountain in the distance. Although you can't see the check dams in the canyon, the Puebloans dryland-farmed the mesa top that the trail takes you across.

At 270 feet (82 m), you can see Horseshoe Tower on the right-hand side. At just shy of 0.1 mile (0.2 km), follow the cairns up a short hill. Once you are up on the hill, the tower comes into a clearer view. Wildflowers are abundant in the brush, including flowering cactus and beavertail prickly pear.

The trail winds through Hackberry Canyon.

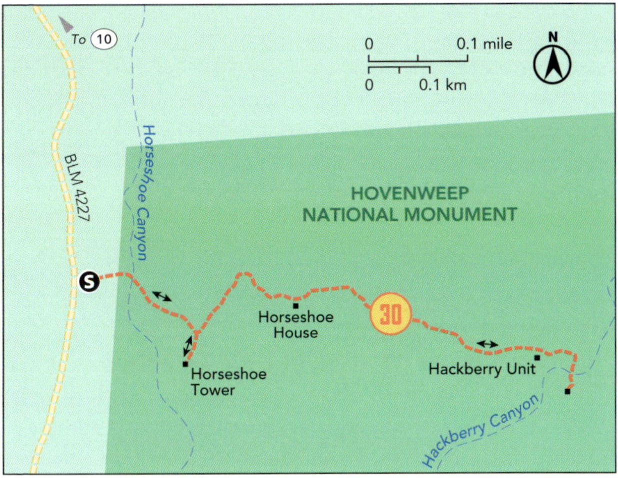

Keep following the cairns along the slickrock trail around the edge of Hackberry Canyon. On the top of Cajon Mesa, sage and juniper allow hiding places for collared lizards. At a bit shy of 0.2 mile (0.3 km), head right on a short side trail to see Horseshoe Tower. Since it is built on a point, the Puebloans could easily have seen into Hackberry Canyon. Looking at the tower, do you see the importance of such a structure for defense?

After seeing the tower, backtrack to the main trail and turn right to continue. Coming into view at a bit past 0.2 mile (0.3 km), you can see what is still viewable of the Horseshoe group off to the right. At 0.3 (0.5 km), the trail leads you to the structures still standing at the group. Can you define the horseshoe shape of Horseshoe House? The four masonry structures create a horseshoe shape (more D shaped), hence the name of the group.

Drainages from springs help vegetation to continue growing where the structures are. Archaeologists believe that the canyon area hosted the densest populations of Ancestral

Puebloans in the Hovenweep National Monument area due to the availability of water. You can still see the density of these villages, supporting archaeologists' suggestions that more than three hundred Puebloans may have lived here at one time.

As you continue through the canyon, the trail takes you through areas of piñon pine, juniper, Mormon tea, and flowering barrel cactus. A wooden sign at almost 0.4 mile (0.6 km) denotes the route to the Hackberry Unit. Less than 0.25 mile (0.4 km) after this point, a small rise has a view of structures that are a part of this group.

What remains of the Hackberry site are structures at 0.6 mile (0.9 km) and about 300 feet (91 m) beyond. The Hackberry group is named for the hackberry tree that continues to thrive here despite the desert-like conditions. Can you spot it as you take in the site? The berries are edible in case you want to grab a quick snack.

Although this area may have had the biggest population, few structures remain after years of erosion. Along the trail, piles of rubble denote a once-standing structure. Can you see the use of chinking stones in the masonry? These stones filled in gaps, a common technique in Ancestral Puebloan architecture. After a storm, you may observe several potholes of water. Enjoy these sites in peace unless the ravens are cawing.

Follow the trail downhill, and up on the right-hand side there are two more houses to observe. An official trail-end sign at 0.7 mile (1.1 km) means it is time to turn around and retrace the same steps that the Ancestral Puebloans once took across the Cajon Mesa top as you return to the trailhead.

ACKNOWLEDGMENTS

To my daughter, Emma, who quite often was my hiking buddy throughout this journey over several years: thanks for being by my side. To my husband, AJ, for buying me a new laptop to write my second guidebook and for always making it work when I need to take a book trip.

Thank you to the staff at Mesa Verde National Park, Hovenweep National Monument, and Canyons of the Ancients National Monument for being so friendly and open to finding answers to some of the more difficult and obscure questions I posed during the book writing process. A very special thanks needs to be said to compliance archaeologist Steven Sundjordet, who led Emma and me on tours through the sites at Mesa Verde National Park during Covid restrictions.

APPENDIX A: RESOURCES

BUREAU OF LAND MANAGEMENT

www.blm.gov

Colorado: Southwest District Office

Open 8 AM to 4:30 PM Monday through Friday
2465 S. Townsend Ave., Montrose, CO 81401
(970) 240-5300

Utah: Monticello Field Office

Open 8 AM to 4:30 PM Monday through Friday
365 N. Main St., Monticello, UT 84535
(435) 587-1500

CANYONS OF THE ANCIENTS NATIONAL MONUMENT

www.blm.gov/programs/national-conservation-lands/colorado/canyons-of-the-ancients

Canyons of the Ancients Visitor Center and Museum

Open March 1 to October 31: 9 AM to 5 PM Tuesday through Sunday; November 1 to February 28: 9 AM to 4 PM Thursday through Saturday; closed New Year's Day, Thanksgiving Day, Christmas Day
27501 CO 184, Dolores, CO 81323
(970) 882-5600

OPPOSITE: *Some of the Lowry Pueblo's forty rooms and eight kivas (Hike 24) are under a roof for preservation.*

GUIDED SERVICES

Durango River Trippers
360 S. Camino del Rio, Ste. 200, Durango, CO 81301
(970) 236-7256

Southwest Colorado Canyons Alliance
PO Box 113, Cortez, CO 81321
(970) 239-1730

HOVENWEEP NATIONAL MONUMENT

www.nps.gov/hove/index.htm

Hovenweep Visitor Center

Open April 21 to November 30: 9 AM to 4 PM Thursday through Monday; December 1 to April 20: 10 AM to 3 PM Thursday through Sunday; closed New Year's Day, Thanksgiving Day, Christmas Day
Located on McElmo Route, Cortez, CO 81321
(970) 562-4282

MESA VERDE NATIONAL PARK

www.nps.gov/meve/index.htm

Mesa Verde National Park Visitor and Research Center

Open 8:30 AM to 4 PM daily; closed New Year's Day, Thanksgiving Day, Christmas Day
PO Box 8, Mesa Top Ruins Rd., Mesa Verde, CO 81330
(970) 529-4465

Chapin Mesa Archaeological Museum

Open May 2 to October 22: 8:30 AM to 4:30 PM daily; October 23 to May 1: 10 AM to 3 PM daily; closed New Year's Day, Thanksgiving Day, Christmas Day
Located on Mesa Top Ruins Rd.
(970) 529-4465

CAMPING AND TOURS

www.recreation.gov; (877) 444-6777

Cedar Tree Tower: open 8 AM to sunset daily; winter: may close due to road conditions

Cliff Palace Loop Road: open late spring to December 1 (or first significant snowfall); 8 AM to sunset daily; winter: closed

Wetherill Mesa: open 8 AM to sunset daily; winter: closed

Step House: open Memorial Day weekend to Labor Day; ranger hours: 9 AM to 3:45 PM

Far View Sites, Mesa Top Loop Road: open 8 AM to sunset late spring to December (or first significant snowfall)

SOUTHWEST COLORADO

Hawkins Preserve

Open sunrise to sunset daily
1500 S. Cedar St., Cortez, CO 81321
(970) 565-1151
www.cortezculturalcenter.org/hawkins-preserve/

Mancos State Park

www.cpw.state.co.us/placestogo/parks/Mancos/Pages/default.aspx
camping reservations (800) 244-5613

Mancos State Park Visitor Center

Open summer: 8 AM to 4 PM Tuesday through Saturday
42545 Rd. N., Mancos, CO 81328
(970) 533-7065

Mancos Valley Chamber of Commerce and Visitor Center

Open April through October: 10 AM to 3 PM Monday through Saturday
101 E. Bauer Ave., Mancos, CO 81328
(970) 533-7434

San Juan National Forest, Dolores Ranger District Office

Open 8 AM to 4:30 PM Monday through Friday
29211 State Highway 184, Dolores, CO 81323
(970) 882-7296

GENERAL RESOURCES

Adaptive Sports Association: www.asadurango.com
Caltopo maps: www.caltopo.com
Colorado Preservation Inc.: www.coloradopreservation.org
Crow Canyon Archaeological Center: www.crowcanyon.org
Gaia GPS: www.gaiagps.com
Great Outdoors of Colorado: www.goco.org
Hummingbird Monitoring Network: www.savehummingbirds.org
Mesa Verde Backcountry Horsemen: www.mesaverdehorsemen.com/index.html
National Forest Foundation: www.nationalforests.org
National Oceanic and Atmospheric Administration (NOAA) weather radio bulletin: www.noaa.gov
Poison Control Center: (800) 222-1222
Seek app: www.inaturalist.org/pages/seek_app
Southwest Colorado Cycling Association: www.swcocycling.clubexpress.com
Southwest Conservation Corps: www.sccorps.org

APPENDIX B: RECOMMENDED READING

Arnold, Caroline. *The Ancient Cliff Dwellers of Mesa Verde.* New York: Clarion Books, 2000.

Baldridge, W. Scott. *Geology of the American Southwest.* Cambridge, UK: Cambridge University Press, 2000.

Childs, Craig. *House of Rain.* New York: Back Bay Books, 2008.

Floyd, M. Lisa. *Ancient Piñon–Juniper Woodlands: A Natural History of Mesa Verde Country.* Boulder: University Press of Colorado, 2003.

Griffitts, Mary O. *Guide to the Geology of Mesa Verde National Park.* Salt Lake City: Lorraine Press, 1990.

Noble, David Grant. *The Mesa Verde World.* Albuquerque: University of New Mexico Press, 2006.

Nordenskiöld, Gustaf. *The Cliff Dwellers of the Mesa Verde.* Mancos, CO: Mesa Verde Museum Association, 1990.

Smith, Duane A. *Images of America Mesa Verde.* Mount Pleasant, SC: Arcadia Publishing, 2009.

INDEX

ABOUT THE AUTHOR

Courtney Johnson lives near Boulder, where she is a freelance writer, public speaker, and educator. She enjoys exploring Colorado and national parks across the United States with her daughter, Emma, and husband, AJ. Her first guidebook, *The Best Utah Children's Hikes*, was published by Colorado Mountain Club Press. Courtney has also contributed to visitor guides for many national parks and outdoor content–based websites.

MOUNTAINEERS BOOKS

SKIPSTONE BRAIDED RIVER

recreation • lifestyle • conservation

MOUNTAINEERS BOOKS, including its two imprints, Skipstone and Braided River, is a leading publisher of quality outdoor recreation, sustainability, and conservation titles. As a 501(c)(3) nonprofit, we are committed to supporting the environmental and educational goals of our organization by providing expert information on human-powered adventure, sustainable practices at home and on the trail, and preservation of wilderness.

Our publications are made possible through the generosity of donors, and through sales of 700 titles on outdoor recreation, sustainable lifestyle, and conservation. To donate, purchase books, or learn more, visit us online:

MOUNTAINEERS BOOKS

1001 SW Klickitat Way, Suite 201 • Seattle, WA 98134 • 800-553-4453

mbooks@mountaineersbooks.org • www.mountaineersbooks.org

An independent nonprofit publisher since 1960

Mountaineers Books is proud to support the Leave No Trace Center for Outdoor Ethics, whose mission is to promote and inspire responsible outdoor recreation through education, research, and partnerships. The Leave No Trace program is focused specifically on human-powered (nonmotorized) recreation. For more information, visit www.lnt.org.

YOU MAY ALSO LIKE